CLARK ASHTON SMITH

Borgo Press Books by STEVE BEHRENDS

Clark Ashton Smith: A Critical Guide to the Man and His Work

CLARK ASHTON SMITH

A CRITICAL GUIDE TO THE MAN AND HIS WORK

STEVE BEHRENDS

THE BORGO PRESS
MMXIII

The Milford Series
Popular Writers of Today
ISSN 0163-2469
Volume Seventy-Eight

CLARK ASHTON SMITH

Copyright © 1990, 2013 by Steve Behrends

SECOND EDITION

Published by Wildside Press LLC

www.wildsidebooks.com

DEDICATION

For Douglas A. Anderson

You and Me Both

CONTENTS

THANKS. 9

ABBREVIATIONS. 10

CHRONOLOGY OF THE AUTHOR'S LIFE (1893-1990) . 11

PART ONE: Clark Ashton Smith: A Reader's Guide to His Work 17

CHAPTER ONE: Overview of Life and Work. 18

CHAPTER TWO: Zothique 43

CHAPTER THREE: Hyperborea 61

CHAPTER FOUR: Averoigne 76

CHAPTER FIVE: Atlantis 84

CHAPTER SIX: Mars 91

CHAPTER SEVEN: Other Weird Fiction and Horrors . . .99

CHAPTER EIGHT: Science Fantasies 111

CHAPTER NINE: Prose-Poems 128

CHAPTER TEN: Verse 133

PART TWO: Seven Supplementary Essays and One Incautious Collaboration 139

CHAPTER ELEVEN: The Song of the Necromancer . . . 140

CHAPTER TWELVE: Clark Ashton Smith & Divers Hands 156

CHAPTER THIRTEEN: The Birth of Ubbo-Sathla 160

CHAPTER FOURTEEN: A Review of *The Devil's Notebook* 168

CHAPTER FIFTEEN: Clark Ashton Smith: Cosmicist or Misanthrope? 171

CHAPTER SIXTEEN: Clark Ashton Smith: Virgin? . . . 178

CHAPTER SEVENTEEN: The Poet Speaks 186

CHAPTER EIGHTEEN: Mnemoka, by Clark Ashton Smith, completed by Steve Behrends 197

PRIMARY BIBLIOGRAPHY 209

SECONDARY BIBLIOGRAPHY 215

ACKNOWLEDGMENTS 218

ABOUT THE AUTHOR 219

THANKS

Quotations from Smith's letters to H. P. Lovecraft, Robert Barlow, and L. Sprague de Camp have been drawn from manuscripts held at the John Hay Library of Brown University. Quotations from the letters to August Derleth derive from manuscripts in the possession of the State Historical Society of Wisconsin.

For permission to publish material by Clark Ashton Smith, I thank CASiana Literary Enterprises, Mr. Richard E. Kuhn and Professor William Dorman. For aiding in the research conducted for this book, my thanks are due Dr. Mark N. Brown, Ms. Barbara A. Filipac, and Mr. John Stanley of Brown University, and Dr. Josephine L. Harper, Mrs. Joanne Hohler, and Mr. Harold Miller of the State Historical Society of Wisconsin. Douglas A. Anderson has made a great many valuable suggestions and contributions to this book. For their support and encouragement in general, I thank Rah Hoffman and Donald Sidney-Fryer.

For This Expanded Edition: My appreciation goes to both Darrell Schweitzer and Rob Reginald. And a special thank you, *in memoriam*, to the earnest twenty-seven-year-old kid who wrote this book, stealing time away from the Tau lepton. He knew more about Clark Ashton Smith than I ever will.

ABBREVIATIONS

AY *The Abominations of Yondo* (1960)
BB *The Black Book of Clark Ashton Smith* (1979)
DC *The Dark Chateau* (1951)
OS *The Double Shadow and Other Fantasies* (1933)
EC *Ebony and Crystal* (1922)
FA *The Fantastic Art of Clark Ashton Smith* (1973)
GF *Grotesques and Fantastiques* (1973)
GL *Genius Loci* (1948)
IM *In Memoriam: Clark Ashton Smith* (1963)
KT *Klarkash-Ton and Monstro Ligriv* (1974)
LL *Clark Ashton Smith: Letters to H. P. Lovecraft* (1987)
LW *Lost Worlds* (1944)
OD *Other Dimensions* (1970)
OST *Out of Space and Time* (1942)
PO *Planets and Dimensions* (1973)
PP *Poems in Prose* (1965)
SA *Sandalwood* (1925)
S&P *Spells and Philtres* (1958)
SP *Selected Poems* (1971)
SS *Strange Shadows: The Uncollected Fiction of Clark Ashton Smith* (1989)
ST *The Star Treader and Other Poems* (1912)
TSS *Tales of Science and Sorcery* (1964)

CHRONOLOGY (1893-1990)

In the following, (s) denotes a story collection,
(p) a poetry collection.

1893 Born (13 January), Long Valley, CA

1902 Moves to Boulder Ridge, two miles outside Auburn, CA

1906 First reads Poe

1910 (Fall) First sale of fiction (Oriental stories in *The Overland Monthly*)

1911 (Jan.) Begins correspondence with George Sterling

1912 (Nov.) *The Star Treader and Other Poems* (p)

1913-1921 Period of ill-health and diminished capacity

1914 First experiments in prose-poetry

1918-1928 Experiments with painting

1918 (Jun.) *Odes and Sonnets* (p)

1922 (Aug.) Begins correspondence with H. P. Lovecraft

1922 (Dec.) *Ebony and Crystal* (p)

1923 (Apr.) "Clark Ashton Smith's Column" begins in *The Aubum Joumal*

1925 (Oct.) *Sandalwood* (p)

1926 Begins correspondence with Donald Wandrei

1927 (Dec.) Begins translation of Baudelaire's *Les Flews du Mal*

1928 (May) Exhibition of paintings at Salon des Independents in New York City

1928 (Aug.) "The Ninth Skeleton" published in *Weird Tales* (first sale of fantastic fiction)

1929 (Fall) Begins fiction-writing campaign, re-reads Poe

1930 (Oct.) Begins correspondence with August Derleth

1931 (Feb.) Plots "A Tale of Gnydron" (genesis of the Zothique series)

1931 (July) Fights brush fire

1932 (Sep.) Begins correspondence with Robert H. Barlow

1933 (Feb.) *Wonder Stories* publishes edited version of "The Dweller in the Gulf"

1933 (Spring) Recommences production of poetry

1933 (June) *The Double Shadow and Other Fantasies* (s)

1934 (Apr.) Meets E. Hoffmann Price

1934 (May) Hires attorney to collect payment for work published in *Wonder Stories*

1934 (July) With Price, collects rock specimens from uncle's abandoned copper mine

1934 (Aug.) Fights wood and grass fire on property

1934 (Nov.) Meets Donald Wandrei

1935 (Spring) Creates first rock sculptures

1935 (July) *Wonder Stories* debt to Smith repaid

1935 (Sep.) Mother dies at age 85

1937 (Mar.) H. P. Lovecraft dies at age 46

1937 (Dec.) Father dies at age 82

1938 (May) Exhibition of sculptures and paintings at Gump's in San Francisco

1941 (Dec.) Meets Robert H. Barlow

1942 (Jan.) Exhibition of sculptures and paintings at Crocker Gallery in Sacramento

1942 (Spring) Sells all but two acres of Boulder Ridge property

1942 (Aug.) *Out of Space and Time* (s)

1944 (Sep.) Begins work on *Selected Poems*

1944 (Oct.) *Lost Worlds* (s)

1948 (Oct.) *Genius Loci* (s)

1948 (Winter) Studies Spanish and begins composing poetry in that language

1949 (Dec.) Completes *Selected Poems*

1951 (Dec.) *The Dark Chateau* (p)

1953 (Aug.) Meets August Derleth

1954 (Nov.) Marries Carolyn Jones Dorman; moves to Pacific Grove, CA

1956 (May) Poetry and prose reading at Carl Cherry Foundation in Carmel

1956 Projects *Far from Time*, (paperback story collection)

1956 Cabin vandalized

1956 (Sep.) Suffers possible stroke (may have suffered others previously)

1958 (Mar.) *Spells and Philtres* (p)

1959 (Aug.) Projects *Cthulhu and Others in Stone*

1960 (Feb.) *The Abominations of Yondo* (s)

1961 (Apr.) Fills in mine-shaft on Boulder Ridge property

1961 (June) Composes "The Dart of Rasasfa" (June-July), his last fantastic story

1961 (Aug.) Dies (14 August) at age 68

1964 (Nov.) *Tales of Science and Sorcery* (s)

1965 (June) *Poems in Prose*

1970 (Apr.) *Other Dimensions* (s)

1971 (Nov.) *Selected Poems*

1973 *Planets and Dimensions* (essays)

1973 *Grotesques and Fantastiques* (artwork)

1973 *The Fantastic Art of Clark Ashton Smith*

1974 *Klarkash-Ton and Monstro Ligriv* (letters to Virgil Finlay; artwork)

1979 *The Black Book of Clark Ashton Smith* (notebook)

1985 (Aug.) Plaque dedicated to Smith, bearing his poem "The Sorcerer Departs," is donated to Auburn-Placer County Library, Auburn, CA

1987 *Clark Ashton Smith: Letters to H. P. Lovecraft*

1988 *The Unexpurgated Clark Ashton Smith* (s)

1989 *Strange Shadows* (s)

PART ONE
CLARK ASHTON SMITH: A READER'S GUIDE TO HIS WORK

CHAPTER ONE
OVERVIEW OF LIFE AND WORK

In the fall of 1930, not long after the onset of his major fiction-writing campaign, Clark Ashton Smith told his friend and colleague, H. P. Lovecraft: "My own standpoint is that there is absolutely no justification for literature unless it serves to release the imagination from the bounds of everyday life".[1] These words lie at the heart of Smith's artistic principles. They were the outgrowth of an isolated, impoverished, dreary, and at times desperate existence, where the only means of escape lay in the exercise of imagination.

For fifty years, Smith's home was a small cabin in the Sierra Mountains of northern California. There he wrote poetry and fiction, painted in water-color, sketched in crayon, and sculpted local rocks into fantastic forms—and there he suffered years of loneliness and hardship. A brief period of notoriety came his way in 1912, at the age of nineteen, with the publication of his first poetry collection; twenty years later, he became a leading contributor to the now-legendary pulp magazine, *Weird Tales* (with H. P. Lovecraft and Robert E. Howard, Smith is often hailed as one of "The Three Musketeers" of *Weird Tales*). But in the main, Smith's work met with little notice or approval. He is known today primarily for his extravagantly imaginative short stories, particularly those set in the fantasy realms of Zothique and Averoigne, and for his exotic science fictions. Though he thought himself a poet for most of his life, his verse resides in

---

1. Letter to H. P. Lovecraft (letter #13, LL), ca. early October 1930.

a handful of small press collections, years out of print, and his artwork has never seen any large distribution.

But whatever the medium of expression, the works of Clark Ashton Smith carry a considerable appeal. Smith was a unique stylist; his writings are artfully crafted, sensual, and rich in color and inventiveness. And taken together, they display an astonishing continuity of theme and image, all the more astonishing when one realizes that his literary output spans a period of nearly fifty years. His ideals, and even certain scenes and settings, remained true to him all his life.

Broadly speaking, Smith's works all share a wish for escape, for a widening of the horizons of experience. His simple and uneventful life bred "a wild aspiration toward the unknown, the uncharted, the exotic, the utterly strange and ultra-terrestrial", an aspiration that "could never be satisfied by anything on earth or in actual life, but only through dream-ventures such as those in my poems, paintings and stories".[2] The realism that characterized the literature of the 1920s and 1930s held no attraction for Smith, for he felt it confined art to "the archives of the ant-hill, and the annals of the hogsty".[3] Thus his "dream-ventures" were strongly at odds with the artistic conventions of his day.

Smith saw himself as an outsider, in his own words "a fantastic, eccentric, impractical, improvident devil: that well-nigh fabulous being, a poet".[4] Born in Long Valley, California, on the 13th of January, 1893,[5] Clark Ashton Smith was the only child of Timeus Smith and Mary Francis (Gaylord) Smith. His British father, who travelled extensively before settling in California (visiting Brazil, Australia, and elsewhere), worked as night-clerk at a local hotel. His mother was born in the Midwest, and sold magazine subscriptions locally to help support the family. When Clark was nine, they moved some six miles to

---

2. Letter to Lovecraft (#15, LL), ca. 24 October 1930.

3. Letter to Lovecraft (#13, LL), ca. early October 1930.

4. Letter to August Derleth, 29 October 1941.

5. Smith habitually gave his birthdate as "Friday the 13th".

a thirty-nine-acre spread on Boulder Ridge (also called Indian Hill), two miles outside the small town of Auburn, and father and son together built the family cabin. Smith described the site as "a rather arid volcanic hilltop [whose] best feature is the wide and elevated view; since, on the west we see a long stretch of the Sacramento Valley and the Coast Range mountains; and on the east the higher foothills topped by more than a hundred miles of snowy Sierran peaks".[6] Certainly he did not lack visual stimulus for his poetic fancy. His childhood was uneventful (as was all his life), though marred by illnesses and a sense of isolation brought on by the remoteness of the family's homestead.

He attended the local grammar school for the required years, though high school was bypassed in favor of an education at home. He later judged that his education really began "with the reading of *Robinson Crusoe* (unabridged), *Gulliver's Travels*, the fairy tales of Anderson and the Countess D'Aulnoy, *The Arabian Nights*, and (at the age of thirteen) Poe's poems".[7] He is also reported to have read *Webster's Unabridged Dictionary* from cover to cover. At the age of eleven, he began producing short stories in imitation of the fairy tales he admired, and poetry soon followed. Four of these early tales, *contes cruels* (biting vignettes) with Oriental themes, found publication in 1910-12.

At the instigation of a local high school teacher who admired his verse, Smith made contact in early 1911 with George Sterling, a well known West Coast poet, who became and remained a friend and supporter of Smith until Sterling's suicide in November 1926. Smith made several trips to San Francisco and Carmel to visit with the elder poet. Sterling also helped in the preparation of Smith's first book of poetry, *The Star Treader and Other Poems*, published in San Francisco in 1912 by Sterling's publisher, A. M. Robertson.

In this collection of verse we see the beginnings of Smith's

---

6. Letter to Virgil Finlay, 27 September 1937 (KT).

7. Letter to L. Sprague de Camp, 21 October 1951.

literary esthetic. As is implied by the title, the scope of these poems is grand and distant, with settings and subjects far outside everyday experience. A handful of pieces take a common beauty of nature as a springboard, while for others the point of departure is some classic myth or figure (classicism was a mark of erudition for Smith). The more characteristic poems of the volume concern celestial matters, including poems to the sun and other stars, an ode to the Abyss, a song of the Comet, etc.

These early poems, rich with imaginative color and evocative metaphor, clearly place emotion over idea. They stand as the first illustration of Smith's lifelong principle that "weighty ideation and application to the problems, acts, emotions of so-called real life have...nothing to do with the true poetic magic, which is wholly a matter of exalted and sublime estheticism".[8] He later applied this dictum with equal fervor to his fiction-writing.

Despite youthful excesses, the acclaim for Smith's poetry was widespread, and he was hailed variously by the San Francisco newspapers as "Auburn's Precocious Genius", "Keats' Equal", and a "New Shelley". This early acclaim enabled Smith to publish some of his work in established journals, such as *The Yale Review*, *Poetry*, and H. L. Mencken's *The Smart Set*. And in June 1918 the Book Club of California published a small collection of Smith's verse, under the title *Odes and Sonnets*.

Sadly, this literary notoriety did little to change what Smith saw as his dull and tedious life. Possibly in reaction to this situation, Smith's stability faltered. From 1913 to 1921, he suffered what he later described as "nervous breakdown and incipient t.b."[9]; and during these years he was feeble and undernourished: at 5 feet 11 inches in height, his weight dropped to 100 pounds, some forty pounds less than his normal weight. He escaped the 1917 draft as a consequence.

Around 1918 Smith took up painting and drawing, without instruction or training beyond what he might have had in

---

8. Letter to Derleth, 5 September 1934.

9. Letter to Derleth, 29 October 1941.

grammar school. He worked in pencil, pen, crayon, and watercolor, illustrating images from his own fancy, his poetry, and, later, scenes from Lovecraft's stories as well as from his own fiction.[10] Estimates of the number of pieces produced run into the hundreds; his letters to the poet Samuel Loveman, as well as those to other correspondents, often included one or two demonic profiles. Though amateurish in execution, his pictorial work otherwise parallels his literary work: the landscapes and figures he produced are fantastically imaginative and make a rich use of color. *The Fantastic Art of Clark Ashton Smith* (1973) and *Grotesques and Fantastiques* (1973; this latter book consists solely of pieces from the Loveman letters) give us a glimpse into this facet of Smith's artistic life, but unfortunately the illustrations in both collections are in black and white, and much of the charm of Smith's works is to be found in his use of color. There remain technical difficulties to reprinting the artwork as well, for the drawing paper Smith used, which was often cheap and coarse, together with his use of the crayon medium, has given certain works a subtle, almost pointillist quality that is lost in reproduction.

By the summer of 1922, Smith was corresponding with H. P. Lovecraft, who was then just beginning to write the many stories of weird fiction which would later bring him great renown, albeit posthumously. In Lovecraft, Smith found a kindred spirit; over the years of their correspondence, which continued until Lovecraft's death in 1937, they greatly encouraged each other in their respective literary pursuits.

Later in 1922 Smith published, at his own expense and through the auspices of the local newspaper *The Auburn Journal*, the second major collection of his poetry, *Ebony and Crystal*. This volume contains less of the cosmicism and grandeur of *The Star Treader*, and on the whole its emotions are

---

10. "The Weaver in the Vault," "The Charnal God," "The Death of Malygris," "The Colossus of Ylourgne," "Xeethra," and "The Seven Geases" each appeared in *Weird Tales* magazine with pen-and-ink illustrations by Smith.

truer to the everyday experiences of a sensitive young man. Much later Smith was to admit that "many years, emotions, sensations, inspirations"[11] found their expression in *Ebony and Crystal*. The outstanding exception to these more earthbound productions is "The Hashish-Eater, or The Apocalypse of Evil", an extensive (576-line) narrative poem of unbridled imagination. The collection also includes a selection of prose-poems, works in a genre that represented for Smith the epitome of prose writing.

To partially defray the printing costs for *Ebony and Crystal*, Smith wrote a column for *The Auburn Journal* consisting of poems and sharp-tongued epigrams. The incongruity of the poet and his surroundings is superbly embodied by these contributions to the newspaper: Hal Rubin has noted that "a *Journal* reader often encountered lines like, 'Seal my lips on throat and bosom fair', on the same page as an ad for Cohen's muslin undergarments".[12]

"Clark Ashton Smith's Column" lasted a little under three years. At about this time, he began a study of French and experimented in writing French verse. Over the next few years, Smith also wrote a handful of undistinguished, non-fantastic short stories, dealing in an ironic fashion with commonplace social situations. Only one ("Something New") was published during his lifetime. And late in 1927, he began a translation of Baudelaire's volume of poetry, *Les Fleurs du Mal*, though he had little prospect of ever seeing it published.

In the summer of 1929, when his then-girlfriend Genevieve Sully demanded that he give up his idleness and apply himself to something renumerative, Smith chose to work at writing imaginative fiction. Over the next four years, he wrote some one hundred short stories and novelettes that he sold to the monthly pulp magazines, particularly to *Weird Tales*, edited

---

11. Letter to Derleth, 20 December 1930.

12. Hal Rubin, "Clark Ashton Smith—Ill-fated Master of Fantasy" (see Sec. Bib.).

by Farnsworth Wright, and to *Wonder Stories*, edited by Hugo Gernsback. To *Wonder Stories*, Smith contributed some very original and then-controversial science fiction. As an author of fantasy and science fiction, Smith hoped to obtain both the independence of means and freedom of imagination he needed constitutionally; and at no point did he doubt his ability to succeed at this new vocation. In a revealing comment to the fledgling writer August Derleth, he stated that "any good poet can always write good prose, if he wants to". We shall see, however, that Smith's own idea of "good prose" was highly idiosyncratic, though entirely in keeping with his imaginative esthetic.

At the time of his entry into fiction, Smith re-read Poe's macabre tales, and read most of Lovecraft's stories from manuscripts loaned by their author. The reading and writing of weird fiction became "an imaginative escape from the human aquarium—and moreover, a 'safety-valve' to keep [Smith] from blowing up and disrupting the whole countryside".[13] After a year or so of fiction-writing, Smith had nearly ceased to think of himself as a poet, and told his correspondents: "my main possibilities henceforward are in prose",[14] and "I am finding a pleasure in fiction-writing and deriving a mental 'kick' from it which I seldom got from poetry".[15]

All of Smith's short stories demonstrate an overriding concern with atmosphere, sensuality, and imagination, with plot and character development greatly deemphasized or completely absent. Smith's stress on mood, at the expense of action, made his stories difficult to market, and he often complained that his finest stories gathered the most rejection slips.

Smith continued to write fiction at what was for him a remarkable rate—averaging almost three stories per month—

---

13. Letter to Lovecraft (#20, LL), ca. 27 January 1931.

14. Letter to Derleth, 25 March 1932.

15. Letter to Derleth, 22 November 1936; letter to Lovecraft (#20, LL), ca. 27 January 1931.

until 1933, when a number of frustrations and distractions reached a critical point. In addition to a growing impatience with the constraints imposed by his editors, he had a falling-out with *Wonder Stories* in February over his story, "The Dweller in the Gulf" (we shall discuss this later), and as a result one of his most receptive markets was closed to him. The worsening health of his aging parents, to whom he was devoted, began to take a heavier toll on both his time for writing and his nerves. He also chose this period to issue, at his own expense, a pamphlet of his best unpublished tales, *The Double Shadow and Other Fantasies*. From February to June 1933 he was engaged in the tiresome aspects of its production, and he soon judged the venture "ill-omened and disastrous".[16] At nearly the same time, Smith fell prey to the lure of his old love, poetry: in May, Smith was asked by George Work, author of the novel *White Man's Burden*, to prepare a selection of his poetry for possible publication in Britain. The project came to nothing, but as Smith became involved in the revising of his old work, his interest rekindled and new poems soon followed. Smith reasoned that "a brief layoff from fiction may be a good thing".[17]

When these difficulties and distractions were behind him, others took their place. In August 1933, Smith's mother overturned a pot of tea upon herself and was confined to bed for months, with all the household chores falling to her son. Her health continued poor, and she died in May 1935 at the age of eighty-five. Smith's father followed her in December 1937, after Smith had spent several terrible weeks "keeping him alive with wine and liquor".[18] And Howard Phillips Lovecraft, perhaps Smith's greatest source of encouragement, passed on earlier in the year.

---

16. Letter to Lovecraft (#39, LL), ca. late February 1934. The edition of one thousand copies cost Smith $125. Over six hundred copies were left unsold by 1937, and many of the absent four hundred had been presentation copies given to friends and neighbors.

17. Letter to Derleth, 23 May 1933.

18. Letter to Robert H. Barlow, 5 December 1937.

Once again, amidst his troubles, Smith found a pleasant diversion. In the spring of 1935, he discovered that some small colorful stones, which he had collected a year earlier with fellow pulp-writer E. Hoffmann Price, could easily be carved into demonic heads and busts. Smith filled his few idle hours with this new hobby, and by his own estimate, he had carved over two-hundred pieces by the mid 1940s.

Smith had always found writing prose especially difficult. His habitual recastings and revisions demanded "long grueling, sweaty hours to get anything done even half-way satisfactorily", whereas painting and sculpture were "child's-play by comparison".[19] Now Smith seemed to lack the time, energy, and forbearance for fiction-writing, and for dealing with the stresses and disappointments involved in the marketing of his works.

All of these many and varied factors seem to have contributed to what was nearly a complete cessation from fiction-writing on Smith's part. Though after 1937 Smith lived for twenty four more years, he finished only sixteen more stories.

His ordeals had drained Smith emotionally, physically, and financially. He drank to excess, complaining of "nerve fatigue" and a sort of general intolerance that he called a "disgust mechanism". And though he was thoroughly sick of his solitary life ("it is killing me by inches", he wrote in 1944[20]) and had a strong desire to leave California—and perhaps even the U.S.— he remained in the Auburn cabin.

With no further checks forthcoming from *Weird Tales*, his financial situation worsened, and he suffered several extremely poor years. In 1942, to pay off the debt incurred by his father's funeral, he sold all but two acres of his Boulder Ridge land. Later that same year he tried for a job at Southern Pacific Rail but was turned down because of high blood pressure. He took to selling his sculptures by mail, and from time to time he marketed a new poem. World War II brought him a summer

---

19. Letters to Derleth, 26 September 1931 and 13 May 1937.

20. Letter to Derleth, 22 October 1944.

supply of orchard and ranch work, but after 1945 Smith's life had bleak and desperate moments. In November 1948, he wrote to Donald Wandrei, saying: "the last two years have been rather hellish ones for me, since I have had had almost no money to live on, and have been stone broke for weeks at a time. Oct. 1947 was the worst period".[21] In the winter of 1950, he could not even afford postage stamps.

The monotony of his life was broken only by love affairs, and visits from friends, correspondents, and fans of his work. Notable is the special friendship he shared with dancer Madelynne Greene and her husband, the poet Eric Barker, out of which grew Smith's cycle of love poems, "The Hill of Dionysus". Between 1940 and the early 1950s Smith met fellow writers August Derleth, Donald Wandrei (whose first visit had been in 1934), Robert H. Barlow, Henry Kuttner, Jack Williamson, Edmond Hamilton, and Fritz Leiber; he may even have met Philip K. Dick sometime in 1954 or 1955. Numerous fans also made the pilgrimage to Auburn, notably Francis Laney and Rah Hoffman, editors of the famous early fanzine, *The Acolyte*; as a result of these visits the magazine published several items by Smith, including excerpts from the *Black Book*, his playfully-named literary notebook.

During the 1940s, Smith taught himself Spanish and became proficient enough to write verse in that language. He also seems to have indulged in the study of magic and, occasionally, in its practice, though little is known on this score. One anecdote, however, relates a strange rite performed by Smith on the tarmac of the small airfield built near his former property: clad only in a nightshirt, Smith is said to have conducted a stately dance late one evening, complete with obeisances to the Four Quarters.[22]

The most important event for Smith in the 1940s was the decision by Arkham House Publishers, a firm founded by his friends Derleth and Wandrei to preserve the work of H. P. Lovecraft in

---

21. Quoted in Donald Wandrei's letter to Derleth of 8 November 1948.

22. Hal Rubin, "Clark Ashton Smith—Ill-fated Master of Fantasy" (see Sec. Bib.)

book form, to issue collections of Smith's own short stories. *Out of Space and Time* was released in a one-thousand copy edition in August 1942 and had sold out by June 1944.[23] It was followed by five others, three of which appeared during Smith's lifetime. Smith also worked to compile his *Selected Poems* for Arkham House from 1944 to 1949, although this did not see print until 1971; the delay in its publication prompted Derleth to issue two small interim collections of poems, *The Dark Chateau* (1951) and *Spells and Philtres* (1958).

Smith's solitary life took an abrupt turn late in 1954, when the Barkers (to whom he had dedicated his *Selected Poems*) introduced him to Carolyn Jones Dorman, a divorced mother of three living in Pacific Grove, California. They were wed a few months later, and by the end of the year the two had moved into Carol's home, although the Auburn cabin was kept as a retreat. Clark spent the remaining seven years of his life in Pacific Grove (called "Piggy" by the couple), half a block from Monterey Bay, with a one-way telephone and $106 coming in monthly from Social Security, his health steadily declining. Some reports have it that he suffered a stroke in Auburn in 1952 or 1953, and by his own admission he experienced an attack of "heat prostration and nervous exhaustion"[24]—very possibly a stroke—after some odd-job gardening in September 1956. That same year saw the first attack of vandalism on the Auburn cabin, which culminated a few years later in its complete destruction by fire.

In May 1956 Smith gave a prose and poetry reading in nearby Carmel, which he advertised as "An evening in the land of Poe, with Clark Ashton Smith, poet-dean of American Science Fiction and tales of the supernatural"; but the life of the "poet-dean" was ending in obscurity, penury, and feebleness.

In April 1961 the Smith's were compelled under court order to fill in an old mining shaft on the Auburn property, dug by

---

23. The title of the collection came from August Derleth. Smith had suggested *The End of the Story and Other Tales*, *Warlocks and Others*, *The Book of Lost Worlds*, and *Planets and Dimensions* as possible titles.

24. Letter to an unknown correspondent, never mailed, ca. February 1957.

father and son, that had been used in later years as a food cellar. Carol Smith describes the affair:

> We worked a week or 10 days ourselves—then [brought in] the bulldozer (driven at 1/4 the cost, by a son of the man who, Ashton said, "sat with me the night my father died, brought me a load of firewood, too"). However, as the bulldozer started the first fill, Ashton stepped forward, and would have been hit had I not stopped him. I knew then, he was, as we crudely say, "not long for this world". [25]

Smith was deeply hurt by this incident, which he no doubt saw as a desecration of his past. After their return to Pacific Grove, Carol became convinced that Smith was consciously setting his affairs in order and preparing himself for death. Five months later, on August 14, 1961, Clark Ashton Smith died of a stroke at the age of sixty-eight.

In December, Smith's cremated remains were buried in an urn, beside what was left of his Auburn cabin; the grave was more permanently settled in August 1962, when his ashes were placed beneath a lichen-spotted boulder.

Some years later Carol Smith married Frank Wakefield, the artist responsible for the cover of Smith's 1948 story collection, *Genius Loci*. She died of cancer in January 1973; her fictionalized biography of Clark, *The Man Who Walks the Stars*, had barely gone beyond the contents page.

* * * * * * *

Smith began and ended his literary career as a poet, while his venture as a professional fiction writer spanned a period of less than ten years. Yet, it is this latter work for which he is remembered today and which has exerted the greatest influence on his

---

25. Letter from Carol Smith to Rah Hoffman, 15 September 1961.

contemporaries and successors, and it is arguable that in fiction his voice is the most distinctive. In poetry, Smith descended from the lineage of Ambrose Bierce and George Sterling (though, of course, Smith's verse is marked by his own striking imagination), but his fantasies and the best of his science fictions mine new ground: he remained a poet while writing short stories, and held himself to the standards of a poet rather than to those of a yarn-spinner. Though the wings of his fancy were often clipped by market-minded editors, his obstinate disregard for conventional standards of plotting and development, and his meticulous concern for the construction of atmosphere and emotional tone, distinguish Smith from the other fantasists of his time.

Smith's interest in prose lay in the glittering surface of the writing, not the intellectual or thematic depths. He reveled in exoticism and the ultra-human, in coined names, in descriptions of unearthly flora and strange, vapor-hung sunsets. An early critic, Arthur Hillman, wrote that "Clark Ashton Smith may be a Prophet of Doom, but he is robed in hues of gorgeous purple and gold. Although the fatalistic acceptance of the utter inhumanity [of the universe] runs like a somber thread through his tapestries, all are beautiful".[26] Carrying this imagery further, Smith might be likened to a maker of fine carpets (of the flying variety, to strain the metaphor), who, to insure the sale of his product at times employed conventional patterns, but whose delight came from the rich color of his thread and the delicate perfection of his weave.

His prose writings partake of skills developed earlier as a poet. A favorite technique involved the heavy use of metaphor and simile, by which an object or scene is likened to something of purer or more intense emotional content. Smith's preference was to describe what something is *like*, rather than what it *is*, forsaking realism and exactitude for emotional power. As a result, his descriptive passages are imbued with meaning, and are *evocative* in the true sense of the word. The interplay

---

26. Arthur Hillman, "The Lure of Clark Ashton Smith" (review of *Genius Loci*), *Fantasy Review*, February-March 1949.

of descriptions with story-lines, or the tensions underlying his scenes, ranges from the obvious (a wizard preparing to announce his curse is said to have lips "like a pale-red seal on a shut parchment of doom"[27]) to the more subtle (a group of dead sailors, the victims of an arctic demon, stare with eyes "like ice in deep pools fast frozen to the bottom"[28]). And occasionally, the use of metaphor enables a description to presage or contain within itself some future scene or happening. For example, in "The Voyage of King Euvoran" a necromancer causes a stuffed bird to fly from the crown of a king and to head out over the orient sea; the utterance that accomplishes this reanimation is "shrill and eldritch as the crying of migrant fowl that pass over toward unknown shores in the night".

These and other literary techniques were employed to establish a definite atmosphere for each of the stories. Smith likened his authorial role to that of a sorcerer: he believed he was practicing a "verbal black magic...of prose-rhythm, metaphor, simile, tone-color, counter-point, and other stylistic resources, like a sort of incantation".[29] The resulting prose-style (like the somewhat similar style of contemporary author Jack Vance) is instantly recognizable, and so great is the degree of continuity in Smith's writing that prime examples of this prose-style are easy to come by. But Smith himself gave us an explicitly characteristic—and deliberately self-parodic—exemplar of his writing. In 1934, by which time Smith had established himself as a major fantasy writer, he was asked by *Fantasy Magazine* to produce a characteristic piece of prose. The magazine's editors asked the "top writers" in the field to describe a lit cigarette in such a way that the author's identity would be instantly apparent. Smith's entry reads:

---

27. "The Dark Eidolon".
28. "The Coming of the White Worm".
29. Letter to Lovecraft (#15, LL), ca. 24 October 1930.

> Ignited in the rich and multi-hued Antarean dusk, the tip of the space pilot's cigarette began to glow and foulder like the small scarlet eye of some cavern-dwelling chimera; and an opal-grey vapor fumed in gyrant spirals, like incense from an altar of pagany, across the high auroral flames that soared from the setting of the giant sun.

Included in this exemplary paragraph are an allusion to classical mythology (the chimera), examples of his elaborate vocabulary ("foulder", "gyrant, "pagany"), and two instances of metaphor. And we note that the setting Smith chose for this "Cigarette Characterization" (as the magazine's series was called) is a grand, colorful, and exotic one.

This ornate and erudite writing-style is a matter of taste, and while for some readers the beauty and power of the stories are "part and parcel of the style",[30] others find the prose verbose and obfuscatory ("His complex descriptions border on redundancy and his words merge into uncomfortable, over-extended conceits"[31]). Smith was aware of the peculiarities of his style, but held that it was better in literature "to err on the side of over-flamboyance or exuberance than to prune everything down to a drab, dead and flat level. The former vice is at least on the side of growth; the latter represses or even tends to extirpate all growth".[32] And the use of an arcane vocabulary, he believed, produced "effects of language and rhythm which could not possibly be achieved by a vocabulary restricted to what is known as basic English".[33]

The transition from poetry to pulp-market story-writing

---

30. Stanley Mullen, "Cartouche: Clark Ashton Smith", *The Gorgon*, July 1947.

31. John Jacobs, "Two Reviews" (review of the prose poem "The Mortuary",) *Nyctalops* #8, August 1972 (Clark Ashton Smith Issue).

32. BB, Item 171.

33. Letter to S. J. Sackett, 11 July 1950.

involved only a grudging acceptance of the traditional elements of adventure fiction. In Smith's best and most characteristic stories (such as "The Empire of the Necromancers", "The Last Incantation", and "The Voyage to Sfanomoë"), the role of plot is kept to a minimum, and only in some of his "scientifictional hackwork" ("The Immortals of Mercury", "The Amazing Planet") do we see the helter-skelter dashing-about of heroic main characters, so loved by magazine editors. In the more extreme examples of this abandonment of plot, the 'action' of the story is reduced to the mechanistic fulfillment of some doom, pronounced in detail at the beginning of the piece. Donald Sidney-Fryer, a pioneering critic of Smith's writings, has called this the "effect of inevitability",[34] but in all likelihood it is less an intentional structural technique, employed for its own sake, than a way of skirting complications of plot. Certainly there is little of the unpredictable in Smith's stories, and much of the inexorable. None of his works employ "surprise" or "twist" endings, although many rely on the improbable conjunction of circumstances or on *deus ex machina.*

Because Smith believed that atmosphere was more important than action or characterization in weird fiction, he created a series of story-cycles in which invented backgrounds act as the connecting element, rather than any set of common characters. The settings he developed were distanced from the modem world by time and space—and the farther from the contemporary and commonplace, the more appealing to Smith: "Though I have sometimes written tales with an actual setting, I am more at ease when I can weave the entire web on the loom of fantasy.... No doubt my own preference is motivated by a certain amount of distaste for the local and the modern, and a sort of nostalgia for impossible and unattainable dreamlands".[35] The

---

34. Donald Sidney-Fryer, "The Alleged Influence of Lord Dunsany on Clark Ashton Smith" (see Sec. Bib.). Examples of the kind of story being discussed include "The Last Hieroglyph", "The Tomb Spawn", "Morthylla", "The Weird of Avoosl Wuthoqquan", and "The Return of the Sorcerer."

35. Letter to Virgil Finlay, 27 September 1937 (KT).

stories set in these imaginary worlds are almost never sequels to one another in the conventional sense (Smith preferred to call them simply "running-mates" or "companions" to one another) and are linked only by their occasional geographical or historical references.

The primary story-cycles are those of the far future continent called Zothique, the Medieval French province of Averoigne, and the ancient northern realm, Hyperborea. Lesser cycles include tales set in Poseidonis ("the last isle of foundering Atlantis"[36]) and on the planet Mars. Smith gave each of these worlds or settings its own attributes and characteristics, which he used to generate particular emotional and atmospheric tones. He tailored his composition to support and accentuate these differences: archaisms of language abound in the tales of Averoigne; a formal, ironic, hyperbolic style occurs throughout the Hyperborean tales; and a somber and metaphorically-rich prose is common to the stories set in Zothique.

In addition to the above story-cycles, each of which is defined by a common constructed world or place, Smith created three series that employ the more conventional linkage of a common main character or characters. Two tales have the omnipotent wizard Maal Dweb as the hero ("The Maze of Maal Dweb" and "The Flower-Women"; this pair of stories has erroneously been called the "Xiccarph series", though only the first takes place on this extraterrestrial planet); three stories and one projected story detail the adventures of the space-flyer *Alcyone* and her crew ("Marooned in Andromeda", "A Captivity in Serpens"—published as "The Amazing Planet"—"The Red World of Polaris", and "The Ocean-World of Alioth"[37]); and Smith's

---

36. "A Voyage to Sfanomoë".

37. This series at one time had the potential for becoming extensive. In August 1930, *Wonder Stories* magazine suggested that Smith write a continuing series of stories about the Alcyone's adventures, with a new installment to appear every other month. For various reasons, Smith declined the offer. We note that "The Plutonian Drug" also belongs to the same future cycle, but does not involve the Alcyone.

character Philip Hastane, fiction-writer of Auburn, California, appears in three stories and two projected stories ("The Devotee of Evil", "Beyond the Singing Flame", "The Hunters from Beyond", "The Rebirth of the Flame", and "The Music of Death"). Smith had once considered writing under the penname of Philip Hastane.

Of the five major invented settings, four are doomed: the final continent of Zothique shall suffer the darkening of the sun; prehistoric Hyperborea will perish in an Ice Age; Poseidonis will vanish in the final whelming of Atlantis by the sea; and Mars awaits its eventual desiccation. And of the five, all save Averoigne is a "fallen" land. Here we see a manifestation of Smith's fixation with loss (a major theme in Smith, as we shall discuss), as well as his sense of the impermanence of material things extending to encompass civilizations, worlds, and suns.

This nihilism forms the basis of many of Smith's attitudes, as expressed in his literary work. His writings clearly demonstrate a belief in the insignificance of humanity and human ideals, and the pettiness of our causes and concerns. Humanism was an aggrandizement of trivialities, "a sort of cosmic provincialism; the egomania of the species...the religion of Lilliput".[38] He considered human beings "the stupidest, greediest, and most cruel of the fauna on this particular planet"[39]—even his phraseology reflects his distant viewpoint. On an intellectual level these beliefs made Smith a belittler of human achievements, a profound skeptic of science, psychology, and religion, and a champion of the inviolate wonder and mystery of the universe, which were "the only elements that make existence tolerable".[40] As a fictioneer, he infused his work with an indifference towards human affairs that many editors and readers found difficult to swallow. Characters are rewarded or sacrificed with an astonishing offhandedness, and his habit of

---

38. From an epigram (BB, Appendix II).
39. Letter to Barlow, 16 May 1937.
40. From an epigram, Item 175 of BB.

destroying or debilitating sympathetic heroes was particularly irksome to his editors, especially when no obvious function was served or moral presented. His projections of Mankind's future seldom included the Utopian visions common to the work of his contemporaries; a favorite target for satire was human pride, pretension, and self-importance.

Smith's characters are frequently made to suffer from weariness and ennui, or to yearn for a Lethean oblivion or the peace of death (consider the necromantically-risen giant of "The Colossus of Ylourgne", whose first independent act is to dig itself a vast grave.) In this way Smith presents the notion that emptiness lies at the heart of all things human, that everything we cherish is pale and meaningless. The weariness of kings constitutes an especially delicate vintage, and one for which Smith particularly cared: though all the world is at hand, nothing can be found to relieve the boredom or despair of the king, who has tasted all earthly pleasures and found them wanting. This situation is presented in the prose-poem "Ennui", the short stories "The Garden of Adompha" and "The Flower-Women", and other works.

The question of reality versus illusion arises often in Smith's work, and his early interest in the subject may have acted as a spur to the development of his distant philosophical perspective. He believed humanity to be physically incapable of piercing the veils of illusion and perceiving the world as it truly is. This underscored for him the extent of our ignorance and the falsity of our grand and sweeping claims. The short story "A Star-Change" and the prose poem "The Touchstone" are direct studies of this subject, but many other works at least touch upon the biased nature of our perceptions of the external world, or our equivocal knowledge of reality. While by no means a unique doctrine, Smith's Idealist views were deeply held and bear connections to his other beliefs and convictions.

It is at least plausible to assert that these rationalized beliefs began as an intuitive knowledge gained in fever-dreams. As a child, Smith had suffered vivid nightmares and hallucinations brought about by poor health and scarlet fever. Nearly forty years later, he fictionalized his experiences in the posthumously published "Double Cosmos" (1940, SS):

> "Even in my childhood, I began to suspect that the world about us was perhaps only the curtain of hidden things. The suspicion was born following my recovery from an attack of scarlet fever attended by intervals of delirium. In that delirium...I had seemed to live in a monstrous world peopled by strange misshapen beings whose actions were fraught with terror or menace.... This realm of shadow had seemed no less real than the world perceived by my normal senses; and during my convalescence I believed that it still existed somewhere beyond the corners of the familiar room....

The arbitrariness of the line dividing illusion from substance was one of Smith's primary reasons for ridiculing both the "realist" movement in fiction and the scientific materialism of his day: both venerated the direct and detailed observation of what was for him the "supreme superstition, Reality".[41] "The bare truth about the nature of things may be more fantastic than anything any of us have yet cooked up. I, for one, find it as hard to swallow the dogmas of the physicists as it is to down those of the ecclesiasts.... Five senses and three dimensions hardly scratch the hither surface of infinitude".[42]

As Donald Sidney-Fryer has noted, when Smith wrote to escape the mundanity of 'real life', he worked to attain to "a greater and eternal reality beyond".[43] In his own eyes, Smith was writing of realms only slightly less substantial than the sordid worlds described by John Steinbeck and *The Scientific American*. In fact, he held that his imaginary realms were

---

41. Letter to George Sterling, 4 Nov. 1926.
42. Letter to Lovecraft (#35, LL), ca. Mid-October 1933.
43. Donald Sidney-Fryer, "The Sorcerer Departs" (see Sec. Bib.).

possessed of a certain peculiar permanence: a fragment of poetry from his *Black Book* reads,

> Taught by me, they will
> Reject the fading phantoms called the Real,
> And choose in place of them those other phantoms
> That fade not, being immaterial.[44]

It is natural to wonder what Smith thought lay behind most people's inadequate picture of Reality. In contrast to Arthur Machen or William Blake, who saw the world suffused with the inner light of an unattainable glory, Clark Ashton Smith suspected that the perceived surface of things cloaked some unfathomable abyss, or curtained an impenetrable darkness. Stripped of "the friendly mirages that make our existence possible",[45] Smith saw no reason to believe that whatever lay beneath them—what Michael Moorcock has so brilliantly termed "the skull beneath the paint"—would be at all hospitable or congenial. "It is my own theory that if the infinite worlds of the cosmos were opened to human vision, the visionary would be overwhelmed by horror in the end".[46] He wrote his famous poem "The Hashish-Eater" to dramatize this destructive impact of an unveiled cosmos.

Smith shared his belief in the hostility of the realms "outside" the human universe with his friend Lovecraft. Like Smith, Lovecraft wrote from a viewpoint that was distant, iconoclastic, and generally unsympathetic to human concerns and ideals. This was a manifestation of Lovecraft's "cosmic" perspective, his sense of Earth's inconsequential placement among the stars and the vastness of the universe. His stories center on the encroachment of unknowable cosmic forces and entities into the human sphere, and the devastating effects they have upon an unprepared humanity.

---

44. BB, Item 128.
45. "The Touchstone" (PP).
46. Letter to S. J. Sackett, 11 July 1950.

Smith's own perspective, as we have said, is characterized by a sense of the littleness of Mankind, but this may have evolved more from misanthropy than from the "cosmic" perspective Lovecraft espoused. While Smith's early poems clearly show an awareness of, and interest in, other worlds and suns, one feels that other attitudes were welded to this interest to yield his own distant perspective. Under close examination of his work, Smith's focus is not on the impersonal universe as often as on the foibles, extravagances, and posturings of an absurd humanity. His characters encounter worlds that are frequently more "antihuman" than "non-human" (consider "Marooned in Andromeda", in which an earthman is swallowed by a carnivorous plant and is promptly spat out as unpalatable); his viewpoint seems more hostile than indifferent. In short, for Lovecraft there was the immensity of the astronomical universe, for Smith the lack of kinship with his fellows.

But quite apart from any intellectual or philosophical concerns on his part, a sense of *loss* pervades much of Smith's literary output. His fictional characters are forced time and again to lose someone or something precious, to live ever afterward a life of regret and sorrow; time and again they stray from the path of happiness and strive desperately to refind it. On a grander scale, we are given whole worlds that have "fallen from grace", that have descended from grand heights into worn-out presents. In Smith's verse, emotions of loss frequently color the images he presents: gardens are overgrown, roses stand brown or without petal, a swath of grass where love had once been made is now unruffled and undistinguished. Other poems, such as "Necromancy" (1934; S&P, SP), have loss as their primary concern:

> My heart is made a necromancer's glass,
> Where homeless forms and exile phantoms teem,
> Where faces of forgotten sorrows gleam
> And dead despairs archaic peer and pass:
> Grey longings of some weary heart that was

Possess me, and the multiple, supreme,
Unwildered hope and star-emblazoned dream
Of questing armies.... Ancient queen and lass,

Risen vampire-like from out the wormy mould,
Deep in the magic mirror of my heart
Behold their perished beauty, and depart.
And now, from black aphelions far and cold,
Swimming in deathly light on charnel skies,
The enormous ghosts of bygone worlds arise.

    As with all his verse, Smith adorned this piece with color and imagery (a process he quotes Keats as calling "loading the rifts with gold"[47]), in this case macabre; but the intent of the poem is clearly to generate a mood of relentless remorse and sorrow for the passing of gladness and grandeur. Further examples of Smith's fascination with such emotions are legion, but one may choose to mention the short stories "The Last Incantation", "The Venus of Azombeii", "Mnemoka", and "The Chain of Aforgomon", in which loves are lost or re-sought; "Xeethra" and "The Empire of the Necromancers", in which characters lose some glad and glorious past; "The City of the Singing Flame", "The End of the Story", "The Light from Beyond", and "The White Sybil", in which a glory beyond everyday life is lost. Several prose-poems, including "Sadastor", "Told in the Desert", "The Frozen Waterfall", and "From the Crypts of Memory", also deal with loss in fundamental ways.

    One can speculate as to the factors that led to this sensitivity to loss. Smith is known to have fallen in love with a blond-haired woman named Iris, who died of tuberculosis sometime before February 1923; this experience may have inspired or colored such works as "The Venus of Azombeii" and "The Chain of Aforgomon".[48] Also, the substantial acclaim he had received

---

47. BB, Item 114.

48. Of his published verse, the uncollected poem "Brumal" or "Winter

for his early poetry—which surely turned the head of the then nineteen-year-old Smith—dissipated within a very short time, leaving him at the end a poor and unemployed young man. His early fame may well have looked quite golden to Smith in later years; perhaps he experienced at first hand the type of loss peculiar to child prodigies.

* * * * * * *

In any attempt to discuss the life and works of Clark Ashton Smith, certain particular problems present themselves. In the realm of the short story, Smith created many memorable pieces, but few masterworks—the oft-reprinted "City of the Singing Flame" and "The Vaults of Yoh-Vombis" being perhaps the only agreed-upon entries in this category. What remains are one hundred and ten completed fantasies available for discussion, many of which are of roughly equal merit. There would perhaps be just enough room here to briefly discuss each one. This option being unacceptable, choices must be made. As a result, the favorite stories of some readers are sure to be neglected, and for this we apologize. This is but one many books that could be written towards an understanding of Smith's fiction.

Troublesome as well is the fact that Smith's fiction-writing period was so short that a chronological discussion of the stories is meaningless. Although we note that his later productions (stories from the 1940s and 1950s) are written in a somewhat simpler prose-style than his works from the 1930s, Smith did not greatly evolve as a prose writer.

As for his verse, the huge amount of material Smith produced

Song", which appeared in *The Auburn Journal* in November 1923, was almost certainly written in memory of Iris' passing:

Life is a tale half-told, / Love is a broken song; / Beauty, besought so long, / Is a legend lost and old.

Winter and silence and woe / Have come, like the end of all: / Slowly the last leaves fall / At sunset over the snow.

Here on the darkening wold, / In the bleak wind blown from space, / I recall thy fugitive grace, / And sigh for thy hair's lost gold.

has made it impossible to discuss this important branch of his artistic life in any detail. While stressing the interconnectedness of Smith's literary output, the task of evaluating his poetry is left to future criticism. This *Reader's Guide* will emphasize Smith's fantastic short fiction, although a brief survey chapter on the verse is included.

At the time of this writing, Clark Ashton Smith is twenty-five years dead, his closest friends have followed him, and precious little has been left in the way of autobiographies, memoirs, or reminiscences by which we might come to understand him as an individual. This, of course, presents problems for any analysis of Smith's life and work, and this lack of material may have served to discourage such analysis.[49] Critical appraisals of Smith are indeed scarce, and in addition, many are somewhat limited in scope. Smith was a poetic, emotional writer, and previous Smith criticism has tended to approach his work after the fashion of the work itself: on the whole, writings about Smith have been expressive and appreciative, rather than critical or analytical. By contrast, Lovecraft's stories are precise and veridical, and this has attracted and engendered a like criticism.

But whatever the level of critical recognition—or acceptance—of Clark Ashton Smith's work, it can be said that he accomplished in fiction what he had set out to accomplish. Through the sensual power of his writing, readers can wander for a time through richly colored realms of imagination. In so doing they walk away from the everyday world, and are reminded that the "real world" they have left behind is not the only one imaginable. Smith himself travelled these same fanciful roads.

---

49. Robert Bloch suggests that Smith's relative obscurity—at least when compared to Lovecraft and Robert E. Howard, the two contemporaries with whom he is most often grouped—can be attributed to this paucity of personal information, information that might otherwise have built up the image of an intriguing writer-personality. See Introduction, SS

CHAPTER TWO
ZOTHIQUE

Clark Ashton Smith's most extensive story-cycle is that of Zothique. Its extant and completed stories, in their order of composition, are as follows: "The Empire of the Necromancers" (1932), "The Isle of Torturers", "The Charnal God", "The Dark Eidolon", "The Voyage of King Euvoran" (1933), "The Weaver in the Vault", "The Tomb-Spawn", "The Witchcraft of Ulua", "Xeethra" (1934), "The Last Hieroglyph", "Necromancy in Naat" (1935), "The Black Abbot of Puthuum", "The Death of Ilalotha", "The Garden of Adompha" (1937), "The Master of the Crabs" (1947), and "Morthylla" (1952). In addition to these stories, Smith completed two related items, the poem "Zothique" (ca.1950) and a play in blank verse, set in Zothique, "The Dead Will Cuckold You" (1951).[50]

Smith's concept of Zothique fast appeared, under another name, in the synopsis "A Tale of Gnydron" (1931), which reads as follows: "Gnydron, a continent of the far future, in the South Atlantic, which is more subject to incursions of 'outsidedness' than any former terrene realm; and more liable to the visitations of beings from galaxies not yet visible; also, to shifting admixtures and interchanges with other dimensions or planes of entity". Smith reiterated these early ideas in a letter to Lovecraft,

---

50. Fragments of further Zothique stories survive, such as "Shapes of Adamant" and "Mandor's Enemy" (both SS), as well as synopses for tales both written and unwritten. Smith also considered writing a short weird-erotic novel with a Zothique setting, "The Scarlet Succubus".

suggesting the variant name by which his story-cycle has now become known: "I have heard it hinted in certain obscure and arcanic prophecies that the far-future continent called Gnydron by some and Zothique by others...will rise millions of years hence in what is now the South Atlantic."[51] The name "Zothique"[52] had itself previously appeared in Smith's synopsis for "Vizaphmal in Ophiuchus" (SS), a projected sequel to "The Monster of the Prophecy", outlined in April 1930; yet here it referred to nothing terrestrial, but represented the name of one of the planets orbiting the star Ophiuchus.

Zothique is portrayed by Smith as an ancient and desiccated land, the last home of mankind in the far future; a world on the brink of eternal night, where "over all, the sun was a monstrous ember in a charred heaven";[53] a decadent world of kings, slaves, and necromancers. The sciences, long discarded or forgotten, have given way to sorcery and magic, and to the prophecies and workings of alien gods. "The continents of our present cycle have sunken, perhaps several times. Some have remained submerged; others have re-risen, partially, and re-arranged themselves. Zothique...comprises Asia Minor, Arabia, Persia, India, parts of northern and eastern Africa, and much of the Indonesian archipelago. A new Australia exists somewhere to the south. To the west, there are only a few known islands.... To the north are immense unexplored deserts; to the east an immense unvoyaged sea. The peoples are mainly of Aryan or Semitic descent; but there is a negro kingdom (Ilcar) in the north-west".[54]

In a general sense, Smith's inspiration for this final land

---

51. Letter to Lovecraft (#2, LL), ca. February 1931.

52. This name was constructed by Smith on the analogy of "antique" (letter to L. Sprague de Camp, 24 October 1950).

53. "The Tomb-Spawn".

54. Letter to de Camp, 3 November 1953. The negro kingdom was originally called Dooza Thom and is so named in "The Witchcraft of Ulua" and in an early draft of "The Black Abbot of Puthuum".

came from the Theosophical "ultimate continent" of Pushkara described in H. P. Blavatsky's occult history, *The Secret Doctrine* (1888), but Smith ironically presented Zothique not as a paradise, but as a world of avarice, hardship, superstition, and crude technology. "I doubt if the Theosophists would care for my conception, since the Zothiqueans as I have depicted them are a rather sinful and iniquitous lot, showing little sign of the spiritual evolution promised for humanity in its final cycles".[55] Additionally, Smith's early reading of *The Arabian Nights* and William Beckford's *Vathek,* with their romantic vistas of deserts, caravans, sunset cities, and sense-weary emperors, probably aided in creating the emotional and visual backdrop for the setting. The similarity must also be noted between Zothique and the astonishing world of William Hope Hodgson's *The Night Land* (1912), which Smith himself described as "the ultimate saga of a perishing cosmos, the last epic of a world beleaguered by eternal night and the unvisigable spawn of darkness"[56]—words which could easily be taken as a description of his own story-cycle. However, it appears that Smith first read Hodgson in 1934, after most of the tales of Zothique had been completed and published.[57]

Donald Sidney-Fryer has speculated that "the hot, dry, dun-colored summer landscape of California" also played a role in stimulating Smith's conception of Zothique.[58] The opening paragraph of "Xeethra" is certainly reminiscent of Smith's Boulder Ridge: "Long had the wasting summer pastured its suns, like fiery stallions, on the dun hills that crouched before the Mykrasian Mountains in wild easternmost Cincor. The

---

55. Letter to de Camp, 24 October 1950.

56. "In Appreciation of William Hope Hodgson" (PD).

57. Letter to Derleth, 29 September 1934. Indeed, it was Smith who passed on the Hodgson books (lent him by H. C. Koenig) to Lovecraft, who then added a section on Hodgson to his *Supernatural Horror in Literature.*

58. Introduction to the Smith reprint collection *The Monster of the Prophecy,* (New York: Pocket / Timescape Books, 1983).

peak-fed torrents were become tenuous threads or far-sundered, fallen pools; the granite boulders were shaled by the heat; the bare earth was cracked and creviced; and the low, meager grasses were seared even to the roots".

By the nature of their setting, the Zothique stories are brimming with images of age and decay. They portray the ruin of humanity, the loss of a glorious and more vital past, the end of all earthly things, a time when not the slightest record or memory of our own civilization survives. This is a humbling vision, as Smith had intended it to be.

Certain of Smith's earlier works foreshadow these ideas and others that he developed more fully in the Zothique story-cycle. Some of the emotional and visual elements that distinguish the cycle date back as far as 1912, when the nineteen-year old Smith had a dream of the final hour of the world, in which the sun cooled and reddened. In fact, some of the descriptive images he used in his transcription of the dream ("Account of an Actual Dream-1912" [SS]) sound remarkably similar to those used in "The Dark Eidolon" and "The Empire of the Necromancers", written twenty years later. The poems "The Last Night" (1911) and "Finis" (1912) also tell of the final moments of the world; other early poems reflecting similar moods include "A Dead City" ("Twilight ascends the abandoned ramps of noon / Within an ancient land, whose after-time / Unfathomably shadows its ruined prime"), and "The Balance" ("the devouring earth, in ruin one / With royal walls and palaces undone / ...shall drift, and winds that wrangle through the vast / Immingle it with ashes of the sun"). The prose poems "The Shadows", "A Phantasy", "Sadastor", "The Sun and the Sepulcher", and the famous "From the Crypts of Memory", give visions of aged and dying worlds, as does the later story "The Planet of the Dead", which itself grew out of the last-named prose poem. All these works feature a general ambience of senesance, decay, and impending doom that appealed to the poetically minded, atmosphere-conscious, and somewhat loss-haunted Smith. Richard Stockton rightly observed that Smith "loved to see the light of a dying sun shine on the agate and onyx towers of cities long deserted".[59]

"The Empire of the Necromancers" (LW) was the first of the Zothique stories, completed in January 1932, some eleven months after the plotting of "A Tale of Gnydron"; it was voted the most popular story in the issue of *Weird Tales* in which it appeared. Smith introduced his readers to the realm of Zothique through the following prefatory or incantatory paragraph:

> The legend of Mmatmour and Sodosma shall arise only in the latter cycles of earth, when the glad legends of the prime have been forgotten.... Perhaps, in that day, it will serve to beguile for a little the black weariness of a dying race, grown hopeless of all but oblivion. I tell the tale as men shall tell it in Zothique, the last continent, beneath a dim sun and sad heavens where the stars come out in terrible brightness before eventide.

Two sorcerers are driven into the desert land of Cincor, where they call forth the mummies and skeletons of that realm to be their slaves and raise up the royalty of Cincor as their servants. The resurrected dead live a dim, vague existence, controlled wholly by the commands of the necromancers, but in time a spark of resistance is kindled in King Hestaiyon and Prince Illeiro, the oldest and the youngest of the dead dynasty of Cincor. In the end they defeat the two sorcerers and curse them with an eternal life-in-death. Then, seeking a return to the peace of oblivion, the reanimated dead cast themselves into a fiery pit below the palace.

More so than any other story in the cycle, "The Empire of the Necromancers" is immersed in the particular atmosphere of Zothique. Some of the later additions to the cycle, while set in desert realms or making reference to ruined cities, might have taken place in some other of Smith's imaginary worlds,

---

59. Richard Stockton, "An Appreciation of the Prose Works of Clark Ashton Smith" (see Sec. Bib.).

but Zothique is at the heart of this story. Here the world is "drear and leprous and ashen below the huge, ember-colored sun", and the entire work is rich in poetic images of death and decay. Seeking a way to end their intolerable existence, we are told that King Hestaiyon "searched among the shreds of memory, as one who reaches into a place where the worm has been and the hidden archives of old time have rotted in their covers". Upon hearing that the rule of the necromancers could be overturned and that oblivion could be theirs again, "the dead emperors and empresses stirred, like autumn leaves in a sudden wind".

Imagery and mood are the primary elements of "The Empire of the Necromancers". Indeed, there is very little action in the tale, no setbacks or sub-conflicts, no voyages or revelations. The dilemma of overthrowing an all-powerful pair of wizards is handled not through some clever twist of plot, but through the use of *deus ex machina*. Hestaiyon tells Prince Illeiro of an ancient prophecy which predicted that a doom, "greater than death", would befall the land of Cincor. The prophecy conveniently went on to explain that the weapons to vanquish this doom were to be found hidden deep in the palace vaults; and thus is the rule of the wizards overturned.

In this story, in contrast to many of his other fantasies, wherein heroes are saved or sacrificed almost at random, Smith makes a firm moral judgment against some of his characters. The necromancers are painted in a far from flattering light ("Dreaming of conquest, and of vaster necromancies, they grew fat and slothful as worms that have installed themselves in a charnel rich with corruption"). Smith wishes us to see that the pair deserve the punishment meted out to them, for they have committed what to Smith was a terrible sin: from the unburdening sleep of death, they had brought back souls to the fleshly world. "Called back once more to the bitterness of mortal being [the slaves knew only] a gray, ceaseless longing to return to that interrupted slumber". Smith was sensitive to "the bitterness of mortal being", and chafed against the limitations of mortality; he felt that the only certain escape from the pettiness and littleness of the world was the escape into eternity.

The people of Cincor have lost not only the peace of oblivion, but also the vitality of their past lives. Prince Illeiro "knew that he had come back to a faded sun, to a hollow and spectral world, to an order of things in which his place was merely that of an obedient shadow. But at first he was troubled only...by a dim weariness and a pale hunger for the lost oblivion". Later he is made to feel this two-fold loss more strongly: "Like something lost and irretrievable...he recalled the pomp of his reign in Yethlyreom, and the golden pride and exultation that had been his in youth.... Darkly he began to grieve for his fallen state".

The emotion of loss forms the thematic basis for "Xeethra" (LW), which also takes place in Cincor though at a time when the land is just beginning to become the unpeopled desert of the previous tale.[60] The young shepherd Xeethra stumbles upon an enchanted cavern, one of the subterranean gardens of the Arch-Demon Thasaidon. He eats a fruit from one of the trees, and thereafter his personality is overtaken by an earlier incarnation of his soul. He believes he is Amero, king of Calyz. He journeys in search of Calyz but finds it a leper-peopled desert. An emissary of Thasaidon appears, who offers to restore the past glory of Amero's rule at the price of his soul, but warns him that he must never regret his decision; Amero agrees, and suddenly Calyz is returned to its former splendor.

But after many happy years as king, Amero succumbs to weariness and to ennui. A minstrel appears, who "sang of a place where the years came not with an iron trampling, but were soft of tread as a zephyr shod with petals...the burdens of empire were blown away like thistledown". The king leaves with the singer, wishing for the simple life of a shepherd, and suddenly Calyz again becomes a desert. The minstrel is revealed as Thasaidon's emissary, and Amero/Xeethra is left to wander aimlessly. "Subtly and manifoldly had the Demon tempted him to his loss.... In the end there was only dust and dearth; and

---

60. It is interesting to note that "Xeethra" was composed more than two years after "The Empire of the Necromancers".

he, the doubly accurst, must remember and repent for evermore all that he had forfeited"—his life as a shepherd as well as his kingly reign. Like the resurrected dead in "The Empire of the Necromancers", Xeethra has suffered a double loss.

No further tales are set in Cincor, though Xeethra is referred to in an ode to Thasaidon that precedes "The Dark Eidolon" (OST). The background presence of Thasaidon, Lord of the Underworld, constitutes one of the strongest true linkages of the Zothique sequence, and nearly every story makes some reference to him.

The Arch-Demon makes his only actual appearance, however, in "The Dark Eidolon". Smith felt this particular story contained "some of [his] best imaginative writing",[61] and Donald Sidney-Fryer has likened both it and "The Empire of the Necromancers" to extended poems in prose.[62] "Dark Eidolon" tells the story of the wizard Namirrha, who seeks revenge for having been trampled in childhood by the horse of Prince Zotulla.

Zotulla is now the cruel and jaded king of Ummaus ("His sins were as overswollen fruits that ripen above a deep abyss. But the winds of time blew softly, and the fruits fell not"), while Namirrha has become "a fabled scourge that was direr than simoon or pestilence". The wizard takes up residence in Ummaus, sending nightly spectral manifestations to haunt the king's palace. These hauntings take the form of invisible horses, which each night draw closer to Zotulla. Long in the service of Thasaidon, Namirrha seeks the Demon's aid for his vengeance, but Thasaidon refuses. Thereafter, in a remarkable scene, Namirrha aligns himself with other monstrous entities and plots his revenge.

Zotulla and his court are summoned to a feast at the mansion of Namirrha, where they are served a macabre meal by mummies and skeletons, a meal "spiced with the powerful balsams of the tomb", and farced "with the hearts of adders and the tongues

---

61. Letter to Derleth, 4 January 1933.

62. Donald Sidney-Fryer, "The Sorcerer Departs" (see Sec. Bib.).

of black cobras". The night's entertainment is no less ominous, provided by "she-ghouls with shaven bodies and hairy shanks, and long yellow tushes full of shredded carrion", who begin "a most dolorous and execrable howling, as of jackals that have sniffed their carrion", and satyrs and devils who play "a lament that was like the moaning of desert-born winds through forsaken palace harems".

The spectral horses of Namirrha's earlier sendings are resummoned, their size magnified immensely, and Zotulla is made to watch as his kingdom is trampled down. Still, Namirrha would carry his vengeance further. He removes the soul of Zotulla from his body and stores it in the dark eidolon of Thasaidon. Namirrha takes control of Zotulla's vacant body, and begins to torture Obexah, the king's concubine. Angered by the hubris of Namirrha, Thasaidon gives Zotulla control over the statue, and Zotulla crushes the skull of his own, wizard-animated body, and in so doing dies. (As in "Xeethra", the main character is tragically the cause of his own doom or death). Namirrha then returns to his own body, but Thasaidon befuddles his mind and drives him mad. As Obexah dies, screaming maniacally, the macrocosmic stallions return "to trample down the one house they had spared aforetime".

"The Tomb-Spawn" (TSS) is the simplest of the tales of Zothique and is one of Smith's most effective mood pieces. It is impossible in a summary to convey the atmosphere of doom and decay which the story evokes so well upon reading.

The work is so calculatingly plotless, however, that one suspects it was intended as a direct challenge to his editors. In the first paragraphs, a storyteller in a tavern of Faraad recites the legend of King Ossaru. This king took for his counselor Nioth Korghai, a monster which arrived on earth astride "a fire-maned comet". Dwelling beneath the king's throne-room, the monster thrived for years; and after its death, Ossam surrounded its vault with a protective circle of enchantment. Upon his own death, King Ossaru was also interred in the vault. The storyteller concludes by saying that it had been foretold "that two travellers, passing through the desert, would some day come upon the hidden vault unaware".

The next paragraph introduces two travelling merchants, Milab and Marabec. Smith has one of the pair beg the question by remarking, "It is a good story...but it lacks an ending".

The two set out across the desert to sell their wares, but are attacked by a band of the semi-human Ghorii. They escape and find themselves in a trackless waste:

> The way led through a dying land.... The hills were dark and lean, like the recumbent mummies of giants. Dry waterways ran down to lake-bottoms leprous with salt. Billows of grey sand were driven high on the crumbling cliffs, where gentle waters had once rippled. Columns of dust arose and went by like fugitive phantoms.

Such mood-invoking passages are found throughout the story.

The pair come upon a ruined city and enter what was once a palace; from a crack in the floor comes a sound like sluggishly moving water. Descending to investigate, they are confronted by the undead Nioth Korghai, which has consumed the corpse of Ossam and now wears the king's head beside its own. As they flee the creature, the merchants cross the circle of enchantment and are reduced to dust. Forgetting the existence of the spelled circle, Nioth Korghai / Ossam follows them into dissolution.

In "The Weaver in the Vault" (GL), three soldiers are sent by Famorgh, king of Tasuun, to retrieve the mortuary relics of a royal ancestor from the dead city of Chaon Gacca. They find the tombs empty of corpses and skeletons; and while exploring the deepest vaults, an earthquake brings the roof down upon them. The surviving soldier, Grotara, comes back to consciousness in time to see the Weaver, a strange, glowing, globe-like creature, rise up from a fissure in the floor. It suspends itself above one of his dead companions and begins to feed; in moments, the corpse has been consumed. After feasting, the Weaver becomes a thing of horrible beauty:

> The globe had become enormous. It was flushed with unclean ruby, like a vampire moon. From it there issued palpable ropes and filaments, pearly, shuddering into strange colors.... Now the web had filled the entire tomb. It ran and glistened with glories drawn from the spectrum of dissolution. It bloomed with ghostly blossoms, and foliage that grew and faded as if by necromancy.

The Weaver descends into the netherworlds, but returns in time to devour Grotara's second companion, and, inevitably, Grotara himself: "With none to behold the glory of its weaving, with darkness before and after, the Weaver spun its final web in the tomb of Tnepreez".[63]

"The Weaver in the Vault", "The Tomb-Spawn", "The Dark Eidolon" and "The Empire of the Necromancers" are simple and atmospheric stories, rich in history, legend, and metaphoric description. And in each of them, all their characters are dead by the end of the story. Clearly, sobriety is the prevailing mood of the Zothique series. Typically, if the main characters are still alive by story's end, then their plans have been overturned, their hopes destroyed, or their cities reduced to ashes. These individual judgments and dooms somberly foreshadow and underscore the impending end of *everything* implicit in the setting of Zothique.

A notable exception to such a somber mood is "The Voyage of King Euvoran", the only truly humorous entry in the Zothique cycle. The story is rambling and episodic, and concerns the search by King Euvoran for a certain gazolba bird (a species thought to have become extinct in the dim past), which had previously adorned his crown; as a result of an argument with a necromancer, the stuffed bird had been brought back to life

---

63. This is the scene illustrated by Smith in the issue of *Weird Tales* (January 1934) containing his story.

and had flown off. With a fleet of war-boats Euvoran follows the path of the gazolba across the orient sea, his party suffering several strange adventures. In the end, the king alone is left alive, stranded upon an unknown island, where he subsists by preying upon the hundreds of gazolba-birds that roost there.

In this story Smith took pleasure in mocking the king's beliefs and behavior. In an island jungle, Euvoran was much annoyed by the huge and vicious gnats—"which were no respecters of royalty, and were always insinuating themselves under his turban"; elsewhere, we are told that his crown had "conferred upon him a dreadful majesty in the eyes of the beholders. Also, it had served to conceal the lamentable increase of an early baldness". These satirical comments are presented alongside examples of Euvoran's intolerable arrogance and pomposity (when attacked by huge bat-like monsters which busy themselves with the slaughter of his crew, Euvoran can only complain of their lack of consideration and bad timing: "King Euvoran was wroth at this unseemly turmoil that had interrupted his supper"). But self-importance is not limited to the character of the king. Held captive on the Isle of Birds, Euvoran at one point describes his stuffed crown to the Bird-Lord and is told: "Thou hast owned a most abominable thing, and one that subverteth nature. In this my tower, as is right and proper, I keep the bodies of men that my taxidermists have stuffed for me; but truly, it is not allowable nor sufferable that man should do thus to birds".

This sort of humor and irony is extremely characteristic of the stories Smith set in Hyperborea, and it is significant that "The Voyage of King Euvoran" was originally conceived as a story with that setting, as indicated by the title's appearance in Smith's list of *The Book of Hyperborea* (BB, Item 3). The irony in this story is designed to make a point, and would teach us of subjectivity, of the relative nature of things. We are given the contrasting and incompatible (yet essentially identical) viewpoints of King Euvoran and the Bird-Lord, which stem from excesses of narrow-mindedness. Later in the story, when Euvoran is forced to share an otherwise unpeopled island with a roughly-cultured and ill-kempt castaway, his lordly bearing is humbled in the light of the castaway's equalizing judgment: "Your kingship is a matter that concerns me little, since the isle is kingless, and you and I are alone thereon, and I am the stronger of us twain and the better armed". Even the simple message of the story's last paragraph reminds us that "rare" and "common" are merely relative terms: "Thereafter they shared the isle of gazolbas, killing and eating the birds as their hunger ordained. Sometimes, for a great delicacy, they slew and ate some other fowl that was more rarely met on the isle, though common enough, perhaps, in Ustaim or Ullotroi".

Another variant mood is found in "The Witchcraft of Ulua" (AY), the most erotic of the Zothique tales. In this strangely moralistic story, Amalzain, a young cup-bearer to the king of Tasuun, attracts the attention of Princess Ulua. When the youth fails to respond to her temptations, Ulua, an infamous witch, plagues him with lascivious phantoms. After several days, these phantoms become more grotesque and unpleasant:

> [One] night as he lay sleeping in the moonless hours before dawn, there came to him in his dream a figure muffled from crown to heel with the vestments of the tomb. Tall as a caryatid, awful and menacing, it leaned above him in silence more malignant than any curse; and the cerements fell open at the breast, and charnal-worms and death-scarabs and scorpions, together with shreds of rotting flesh, rained down upon Amalzain.

In an ironic tone, Smith writes that Amalzain "no longer could he read his books or solve his problems of algebra in peace". The youth seeks the help of his great-uncle, Sabmon the Anchorite, who dwells in a desert hut composed of "the smaller bones of wild dogs and men and hyenas" (note man's placement and company in this list). Sabmon dispels the phantoms, and together they watch as an earthquake tumbles the towers of the city wherein Ulua dwells.

In its original form, Smith was unable to sell this story, mainly because of Ulua's temptation scene, which read:

> "I would have you for my lover", said Ulua. "Behold! my arms are the portals of untold raptures and felicities. The pleasures I give are keener than the pangs of a fiery death. The dead kings of Tasuun will whisper enviously of our love to their dead queens in the immemorial granite vaults below Chaon Gacca. Thasaidon, the black, shadowy lord of hell, hearing the tale that his demons bring to him of us, will wish to become incarnate in a mortal body...."[64]

Strangely, Farnsworth Wright, editor of *Weird Tales*, branded "The Witchcraft of Ulua" "a sex story" on the basis of this one scene. Smith contended that "erotic imagery was employed in the tale...to achieve a more varied sensation of weirdness",[65] but in the end he was forced to eliminate this speech, and to replace it with the more innocuous pair of questions: "See you not that I am beautiful and desirable? Or can it be that your perceptions are duller than I had thought?"

Notice must also be taken of Smith's only completed drama, the play in blank verse "The Dead Will Cuckold You" (IM,SS). Set in Zothique, the story-line centers around Smaragad, King of Yoros, and his young Queen, Somelis. A poet named Galeor has found favor with the queen. Smaragad is jealous, and fearing to be made a cuckold, he poisons Galeor's wine, telling him: "You have drunk / A vintage that will quench all mortal thirst. / You will not look on queens nor they on you / When the thick maggots gather in your eyes". Galeor dies, and Somelis curses Smaragad.

The scene changes to the king's audience hall, where Smaragad has summoned the fearsome necromancer Natanasna

---

64. "The Witchcraft of Ulua", *The Unexpurgated Clark Ashton Smith*.

65. Letter to Derleth, 29 August 1933.

(who "Stinks like a witch's after-birth, and evil / Exhales from him, lethal as that contagion / Which mounts from corpses mottled by the plague"). Natanasna admits to the crime of raising the dead, but also recalls the law forbidding murder and challenges Smaragad: "you the king have filled / More tombs than I the outlawed necromancer / Have ever emptied". The king is enraged and orders the necromancer to leave the city.

Natanasna quits Yoros and meets his assistant in a graveyard, where together they perform rites (invoking Thasaidon's power) that cause a demon to invade and re-animate the corpse of Galeor. They order the demon to "seek out the chamber of the Queen Somelis, / And woo her lover-wise till that be done / Which incubi and lovers burn to do". The demon obeys. However, within the Queen's bed-chamber, Somelis calls upon Ililot, goddess of lovers, and Galeor's true self seems to reawaken. He forgets the commands of Natanasna, but ironically will fulfill them, for Somelis wishes to consummate their love: "I am glad to have you, whether dead / Or living.... The grave has left you cold: / I'll warm you in my bed and in my arms".

The play ends with Smaragad burning down the bolted door of his Queen's bed-chamber, thereby setting the entire palace aflame. When the door collapses inward, Smaragad brandishes his sword and leaps forward, crying, "I'll go and carve the lechers while they roast / Into small dollops for the ghouls to eat". It is important to note that Smaragad's arrogance and pride brings his palace down upon his head. His counselors suggest more sensible and less destructive ways of gaining the room, but Smaragad's pride will not permit him to scale the outer wall ("Nor am I a thief / To enter by a window") or order his soldiers to use a battering ram ("I'll not have / A legion here to witness what lies crouched / In the queen's chamber. Nor am I accustomed / To beat on closen doors that open not").

"The Dead Will Cuckold You" is in Smith's own words one of

his "masterpieces"[66]. It is perhaps his most successful merging of story and imagination with poetic style. The play has never been performed and has never had any wide circulation, which is regrettable. This drama is on a level with Smith's best works, and for all its color and exoticism displays an earthiness not often found in his writings.

As in the play above, fully half of the Zothlque short stories concern themselves with the vicissitudes of royal families. The use and misuse of power fascinated Smith, as did the related diseases of ennui and disillusionment. The rulers of Zothique are portrayed as jaded sensualists who seek to be delivered from their ennui by "strange loves and cruelties...extravagant pomps and mad music...the aphrodisiac censers of far-sought blossoms, the quaintly shapen breasts of exotic girls".[67] Richard Stockton once noted that "above all Smith loved 'the ultimate refinement that is close to an autumnal decay', the *decadence* attainable only to those civilizations of such great age as to have their very beginnings lost even in the most remote antiquity".[68]

Smith recognized that the Zothique tales were particularly steeped in excesses of human behavior, describing his first Zothique story, "The Empire of the Necromancers", as "muchly overgreened with what H. P. Lovecraft once referred to as the 'verdigris of decadence'".[69] And examples of decadent behavior abound. In "The Garden of Adompha", the king of the isle of Sotar tends, "with a curious and morbid aesthetic pleasure", a gruesome garden wherein the severed limbs of his courtesans have been grafted to strange, half-animate plants. The king "found in them the infallible attraction of things enormous and hypernatural". In "The Isle of the Torturers", an entire people are given over to a worship of cruelty and pain. A young prince

---

66. Letter to de Camp, 21 October 1952.

67. "The Garden of Adompha".

68. Richard Stockton, "An Appreciation of the Prose Works of Clark Ashton Smith" (see Sec. Bib.).

69. Letter to Derleth, 9 January 1932.

washes ashore on this island, and is taken prisoner and tortured for the pleasure of the inhabitants. During his ordeal, the prince is given reason to hope that a rescue will soon be forthcoming; but this is revealed as a hoax, a refined form of torture in itself. And the debased sin of necrophilia is present in "The Death of Ilalotha" and "The Empire of the Necromancers".

Although in the stories mentioned above, the characters who demonstrate decadent behavior meet grisly ends, Smith was not moralizing. While doubtless Smith objected personally to cruelty, he had no problem with sensuality and hedonism, or to other pleasures of a bizarre nature. In fact, Smith's last story of Zothique, "Morthylla", gives the fullest explanation of his feelings. This story concerns the young poet Valzain; at an extravagant party, he watches "the gala throng that eddied past him... with an indifference turning toward disgust". But Valzain is not passing judgment on the shallowness of the carnal; rather, he is only bored. "'I can taste only the dregs in every cup. And tedium lurks at the middle of all kisses". With a desire to experience something new, to feel the thrill of a new sensation, he becomes the lover of Morthylla, a mysterious woman who calls herself a lamia. They tryst in a forgotten graveyard, and "night after night his disgust and weariness sloughed away from him, in a fascination fed by the spectral milieu, the environing silence of the dead, his withdrawal and separation from the carnal, garish city". Morthylla asks, "Have I not beguiled you from your boredom?" "Kill me with your lips, devour me as you are said to have devoured others", Valzain replies. This yearning for new sensations, which in his science fiction work led Smith to invent new and fantastic sensory equipment, is very much a part of decadent sensuality. And Valzain is not condemned for his strange desires, but instead is rewarded, at the story's end, with an eternal dream of happiness and expectation.

Something should be said here about the chronology of the Zothique stories. Smith wrote the tales in no particular order, but he did link a few of them together through common references;[70] otherwise, any ordering of the remaining stories is entirely arbitrary. Lin Carter's published chronology[71] is for the most part an exercise in imagination. There is no evidence that Smith ever conceived of the Zothique stories in any objective sequence, and it is likely that he would have ordered them for book publication according to their artistic or thematic content.

It is known, however, that Smith intended "The Last Hieroglyph" as the concluding piece for any collection of his Zothique tales[72]. In this story, Vergama, the god of destiny, creates and destroys all earthly things by adding or erasing hieroglyphs from his ledger. After all the main characters of the story are reduced to ciphers in this ledger, the story ends: "Vergama leaned forward from his chair, and turned the page".

---

70. The major internal threads in the story-cycle are the Lunalia-Famorgh dynasty (which relates "The Weaver in the Vault", "The Witchcraft of Ulua", and the fragment "Mandor's Enemy"), the country of Cincor (relating "Xeethra", "The Empire of the Necromancers", and "The Tomb-Spawn"), and the deeds of Namirrha (mentioned in "The Dark Eidolon", "The Tomb-Spawn", and "The Last Hieroglyph").

71. Lin Carter, "Epilogue: The Sequence of the Zothique Tales", *Zothique*, NY: Ballantine Books, 1970.

72. Letter to Barlow, 21 May 1934. On the subject of a Zothique collection, Smith wrote that the stories "could be collected with a brief note as to suppositional geography and chronology" (letter to Derleth, 29 August 1933); it is regrettable that such a note never came to be written.

CHAPTER THREE
HYPERBOREA

The Hyperborean series of stories, consisting of ten completed fantasies, acts in some ways as a foil to the Zothique. One obvious contrast is in temporal setting, for Smith lays these two story-cycles in imaginary continents at opposite extremes of Earth's habitability. Hyperborea is depicted as the earliest home of mankind, a polar land whose northern tip, Mhu Thulan, corresponds roughly with present-day Greenland. Civilization flourished there from the Miocene age, some fifteen million years ago, to the glacial Pleistocene, one million years in the past.[73] The first entry in the Hyperborean sequence, "The Tale of Satampra Zeiros", was written late in 1929; the final entry, "The Theft of the Thirty-Nine Girdles", is a sequel to the first, composed twenty-eight years later. Between these bracketing tales fall "The Door to Saturn", "The Testament of Athammaus", "The Weird of Avoosl Wuthoqquan", "Ubbo-Sathla", "The White Sybil", "The Ice-Demon", "The Coming of the White Worm", and "The Seven Geases". In addition Smith plotted "The Hyperborean City", "The Shadow from the Sepulcher", and "The House of Haon-Dor" as part of the series, and produced a partial draft of the last-named piece.

Partly as a result of the contrast in setting, the overall atmosphere of the Hyperborean series is quite at odds with that of Zothique. The latter stories are steeped in an ambience of senes-

---

73. Miocene times are mentioned in "Ubbo-Sathla", while "The Ice-Demon" takes place during the Pleistocene era.

cence and decay, and all events take place under a pall of weariness and fatalism. Yet, in the days of Hyperborea, the world is new and fresh, the land is fertile and overgrown, and humanity is a relative newcomer. The people of Hyperborea reflect the vitality of their age, for on the whole they are vigorous, greedy, fanatical, pompous, possessed by their self-declared grandeur, and thus differ sharply from the languid and vein-drawn sybarites of Zothique.

Smith had low regard for the egocentric (or anthropocentric) attitudes that his Hyperborean characters exhibit, so it is not surprising to see such attitudes as pride, bravado, and self-righteousness ridiculed in these tales. This ridicule introduces a note of humor that is almost completely absent from somber and doom-filled Zothique; Smith recognized this himself, saying that the Hyperborean cycle stood out from his other work through its "marked ironic content".[74] Not all of this humor was designed to make a point—Smith used the Hyperborean stories as an opportunity to write in a generally funnier vein.

The writing style found in these tales supports the humorous and ironic content. The prose is intentionally pretentious, so as to mock pretension—a technique found more recently in the work of Jack Vance. We encounter elegantly depicted scenes of great silliness, absurd speeches delivered by sagacious characters, humor that is droll, dry, quiet, and above all, *mock solemn.* The escape of the persecuted wizard Eibon in "The Door to Saturn", for example, is presented in the following fashion: "Envisaging in thought the various refinements and complications of torture which [the Inquisitor] Morghi would have prepared [for him], he sprang through the opening into Cykranosh with an agility that was quite juvenile for a wizard of mature years". Even in scenes tinged with horror, Smith's sly smile shows through. In "The Testament of Athammaus", the once-executed criminal Knygathin Zhaum returns to the streets of Commoriom and commits a foul deed: "He had eaten no less a personage than

---

74. Letter to Derleth, 6 April 1937.

one of the eight judges [of his trial]; and, not satisfied with picking the bones of this rather obese individual, had devoured by way of dessert the more outstanding facial features of one of the police who had tried to deter him from finishing his main course".

In certain instances, this particular style of writing serves to diminish the impact and vitality of Smith's work and to lessen its distinctiveness. In the more ironic of the Hyperborean stories, such as "The Door to Saturn" and "The Seven Geases", Smith is guilty of writing the kind of prose his critics habitually accuse him of writing—prose that is verbose, circumlocutious, over-elegant, distant, and non-visual. Smith wrote these stories in a language of formal hyperbole, a language designed to highlight and underscore the pomposity and empty pride of his characters, and the solemn cadence of the prose is meant to contrast with the absurdity of their actions and beliefs. But regardless of the motivations for this style of writing, an unwanted side effect is the loss of the color and sensuality that distinguishes Smith's other fiction, the loss of those qualities that single him out as a poet among writers.

The mixture of humor and horror that characterizes this series was manifest from the start. "The Tale of Satampra Zeiros" (1929, LW) relates an adventure of the two thieves Satampra Zeiros and Tirouv Ompallios, in which they travel to the deserted city of Commoriom, once the capitol of the continent, with the intention of looting it "at the expense of a few dead kings or gods". The ruins retain an evil and sinister reputation, and only their impoverished circumstances convince the thieves to make such a raid. Their journey through the jungle to Commoriom is fraught with anxiety, although relief from their state of mind does not prove entirely elusive:

> Each of us took a liberal draft [of palm-wine], and presently the jungle became less awesome; and we wondered why we had allowed the silence and the gloom, the watchful bats and the brooding immensity,

to weigh upon our spirits for even a brief while; and I think that after a second draft we began to sing.

They reach Commoriom and enter the squat, forbidding temple of the pre-human god Tsathoggua. Within they find a wide basin filled with some black, gelid substance. To their horror, the liquid begins to stir, and from it "an uncouth amorphous head with dull and bulging eyes arose gradually on an ever lengthening neck.... Then two arms—if one could call them arms—likewise rose inch by inch, and we saw that the thing was not, as we had thought, a creature immersed in the liquid, but that the liquid itself had put forth this hideous neck and head". Then begins a nightmare chase through the surrounding marshes with the monster in constant pursuit, a chase that ends hours later back at the temple. Tirouv Ompallios takes refuge in the basin while Satampra Zeiros hides behind a statue of Tsathoggua. Entering the temple, the creature "reared itself up like a sooty pillar...gathering all its bulk in an immense mass on a sort of tapering tail, and then like a lapsing wave it fell upon Tirouv Ompallios. Its whole body seemed to open and form an immense mouth as it sank down from sight". Zeiros attempts to leave the fane as quietly as possible, feeling that "it would be highly injudicious to disturb the entity in the bowl while it was digesting Tirouv Ompallios", but is discovered at the last moment and loses his right hand to the creature.

This story is notable not only for being the first of the Hyperborean tales, but also for marking the first appearance of Tsathoggua,[75] an entity that plays much the same unifying role in the Hyperborean series that Thasaidon plays in Zothique. He is

---

75. The first published reference to Tsathoggua occurred in "The Whisperer in Darkness" by H. P. Lovecraft. Early in 1930, Smith sent the manuscript of "The Tale of Satampra Zeiros" to Lovecraft, who then incorporated Tsathoggua into the framework of the Cthulhu Mythos by mentioning him in "The Mound" and "The Whisperer in Darkness"; and the latter story appeared in Weird Tales before Smith's own tale.

one of the elder gods, who receives no longer any worship from men, but before whose ashen altars, people say, the furtive and ferocious beasts of the jungle, the ape, the great sloth and the long-toothed tiger, have sometimes been seen to make obeisance and have been heard to howl or whine their inarticulate prayers.

This demon god (whose name is sometimes given as Zhothaqquah, Sodaqui, or Sadoqua) is described in the story as "squat and pot-bellied...his head was more like a monstrous toad than a deity, and his whole body was covered with...short fur, giving somehow the vague suggestion of both the bat and the sloth.... In truth he was not a comely or personable sort of god". Smith sketched this initial vision of Tsathoggua on the margin of a manuscript page from the holograph first draft of "The Tale of Satampra Zeiros", and the result is something like a malign Buddha wearing a tasseled crown or skull-cap.[76]

Smith had intended to write a further (and obviously earlier) adventure of Satampra Zeiros and Tirouv Ompallios, but "The Shadow from the Sepulcher" (BB) never went beyond its synopsis. He did complete "The Theft of the Thirty-Nine Girdles" (TSS), however, which tells of a later exploit of Zeiros with his new companion, Vixeela. This slight but enjoyable tale is told in a style that is simpler and more fluid than many of the other Hyperborean stories, reflecting Smith's late-in-life move away from what he felt was the wordiness of his earlier works. He composed the piece during the period 1952-1957, and produced an extensive string of intermediate drafts, several of which begin with the poem "Lament for Vixeela":

> Vixeela, daughter of beauty and of doom!
> Thy name, an invocation, calls to light
> Dead moons, and draws from overdated night
> The rosy-bosomed spectre of delight.

---

76. Used as the cover illustration for *Klarkash-Ton: The Journal of Smith Studies* (Cryptic Press, 1988).

> Like some delaying sunset, brave with gold,
> The glamors and the perils shared of old
> Outsoar the shrunken empire of the mould.

A one-time priestess of the god Leniqua, Vixeela helps Zeiros conduct a raid on the temple's wealth, which consists of thirty-nine golden chastity belts worn by the priestesses. These priestesses are, in reality, a harem of beautiful "virgins" held prisoner within the temple, and each is sold into nightly prostitution by the priests. Don Herron has noted that Smith "used ridicule to point out some of the hypocrisy prevalent in many organized religions",[77] and the humor in "The Theft of the Thirty-Nine Girdles" is aimed at just that target: "It will thus be seen that the virginity of the priestesses was nominal; but its frequent and repeated sale was regarded as a meritorious act of sacrifice to the god".[78]

"The Door to Saturn" (1930; LW) carries on the ridicule of religion and religious intolerance. The story was a personal favorite of Smith's "on account of its literary style",[79] but in truth its prose is some of his most distant and hyperbolic. Designed in part to aid in the lampooning of the zealous and pompous Inquisitor Morghi, the writing style nonetheless works against the tale by reducing the degree to which the reader becomes involved in its events. The story concerns the wizard Eibon, author of *The Book of Eibon*, a magical grimoire mentioned many times throughout the Hyperborean sequence (in fact, "The Coming of the White Worm" is presented as the ninth chapter of this book). He is sought by Morghi as a religious

---

77. Don Herron, "The Double Shadow" (see Sec. Bib.)

78. At times Smith's humor is extremely quiet. The mall Vixeela, an involuntary harlot by night and wearer of a golden chastity belt by day, "had found small pleasure in the religious prostitution and had chafed at the confinement entailed by it".

79. Letter to Derleth, 15 September 1931. "I have a peculiar fondness for this story. I take out the ms. and read it over, when I am too bored to read anything in my book-cases" (letter to Derleth, 20 January 1931).

heretic but escapes to Saturn using magic supplied him by Zhothaqquah. Morghi and his raiding party are disappointed to find the wizard's house empty, "because there seemed to be no early prospect of trying out the ingenious agonies, the intricately harrowing ordeals which they had devised for Eibon with such care".

On Saturn, Eibon meets a creature that he presumes to be Zhothaqquah's uncle, Hziulquoigmnzhah, on the basis of its eating habits: "the creature drank of the (lake of) fluid metal in a hearty and copious manner that served to convince Eibon of its godship; for surely no being of an inferior biologic order would quench its thirst with a beverage so extraordinary". The creature utters three unknown words and departs; Eibon concludes that he has heard some portentous prophecy and has been appointed the god's messenger. Morghi follows Eibon to Saturn and appears on the scene, but the two agree to set their feud aside for a time and travel together. With great solemnity they set out across the Saturnian fields, seeking to deliver the god's message to somebody.

A host of strange peoples and creatures are encountered in their wanderings. At one point the pair are given the opportunity to become husbands to the national mother of a headless race, the Blemphroims:

> Eibon and Morghi were quite overcome by the proposed eugenic honor. Thinking of the mountainous female they had seen, Morghi was prone to remember his sacerdotal vows of celibacy and Eibon was eager to take similar vows upon himself without delay.... The sorcerer temporized by making a few queries anent the legal and social status which would be enjoyed by Morghi and himself.... And the naive Blemphroims told him that this would be a matter of brief concern; that after completing their marital duties the husbands were always served to the national mother in the form of ragouts and other culinary preparations.

They make a hasty escape from the land of the Blemphroims before dinner is served, and during the flight "whenever [Morghi] paused to recover his breath, Eibon would say to him: 'Think of the national mother,' and Morghi would climb the next acclivity like an agile but somewhat asthmatic mountain-goat".

Eventually they come across a people capable of understanding the god's message, which to their disappointment and chagrin translates effectively as "be off with you". What they had taken to be a statement of godly portent was no more than Hziulquoigmnzhah's offhand dismissal.

Eibon and Morghi choose to remain with these people, the Ydheems, although Morghi is not entirely content: "Though the Ydheems were religious, they did not carry their devotional fervor to the point of bigotry or intolerance; so it was quite impossible to start an inquisition among them". The story concludes by explaining that, back in Hyperborea, the disappearance of Morghi had been attributed to the power of Zhothaqquah, and that this had promoted "a widespread revival of the dark worship of Zhothaqquah...in the last century before the onset of the great Ice Age".

This ending reiterates that Hyperborea, like Zothique, is a doomed land, destined to suffer a frozen death beneath mile-thick glaciers. The slow encroachment of this doom is evident within the series as well: lands that are fair in one tale are ice-covered in another. This progression of doom permits a rough chronological ordering of the works in the series, and Lin Carter's conjectural ordering[80] seems an ingenious job.

"The Seven Geases" (1933, LW), like "The Door to Saturn", is a walking-tour through fantastic realms, told in a dry and

---

80. Lin Carter, "Notes on the Commoriom Myth-Cycle", *Hyperborea* (New York: Ballantine Books, 1971). Carter imposes the following order: "The Seven Geases", "The Weird of Avoosl Wuthoqquan", "The White Sybil", "The Testament of Athammaus", "The Coming of the White Worm", "Ubbo-Sathla", "The Door to Saturn", "The Ice-Demon", "The Tale of Satampra Zeiros", and "The Theft of the Thirty-Nine Girdles".

formal manner, and featuring an ironic treatment of a self-important main character. Lord Ralibar Vooz is described as "a high magistrate of Commoriom and third cousin to King Homquat"; it is no accident that Smith juxtaposes the officious title of "high magistrate" against a distant and meager relationship to a humorously named king. Vooz is a stubborn and bellicose bravo ("it was not in his nature to abandon any enterprise, no matter how trivial, without reaching the set goal") who stumbles upon a sorcerer in the midst of an incantation. When berated for his intrusion, Vooz responds, "How now, varlet.... Who are you to speak so churlishly to a magistrate of Commoriom and a cousin to King Homquat? I advise you to curb your insolence", to which the sorcerer replies, "I care not if you are the magistrate of all swinedom or a cousin to the king of dogs". The sorcerer lays a "geis" or curse upon Vooz that compels him to descend into Mount Voormithadreth—home of the sub-human Voormis, the spider-god Atlach-Nacha, a race of ancient serpent-men, and other odd creatures and individuals—and offer himself to Lord Tsathoggua. Once inside the mountain, Vooz is passed along as a gift from entity to entity, and in every case he is looked upon as either a worthless toy or an offering made in bad taste. After his adventures, Smith simply has him fall into a bottomless abyss.

By contrast, "The White Sybil" (1932, AY) leaves the coldly formal prose and ironic asides behind and returns to the poetic, visual prose of Smith's finest work. The emotional and thematic inspiration for this piece comes from two prose poems, "The Muse of Hyperborea", composed late in 1929 (despite its title, this bit of fancy bears no direct relation to the Hyperborean story-cycle), and the earlier "The Traveller". To see this latter connection, check the memorable opening paragraph of "The White Sybil" against the beginning of "The Traveller":

> Tortha, the poet, with strange austral songs in his heart, and the umber of high and heavy suns on his face, had come back to Cerngoth, in Mhu Thulan, by

the Hyperborean sea. Far had he wandered in the quest of that alien beauty which had fled always before him like the horizon. Beyond Commoriom of the white, numberless spires, and beyond the marsh-grown jungles to the south of Commoriom, he had floated on nameless rivers, and had crossed the half-legendary realm of Tscho Vulpanomi, upon whose diamond-sanded, ruby-graveled shores an ignescent ocean was said to beat forever with fiery spume. ("The White Sybil")

Stranger, where goest thou...with thy brow that alien suns have darkened.... Wanderest thou in search of cities greater than Rome, with...fanes more white than the summer clouds, or the foam of Hyperboreal seas? Or farest thou to the lands...lit by the baleful and calamitous beacons of volcanoes? Or seekest thou an extremer shore, where the red and monstrous lilies are like innumerable flambeaux held aloft on the verge of the waveless waters? ("The Traveller")

Like "the traveller" of the prose poem, who seeks in vain the beauty of his former home, Tortha has searched the world for an ill-defined beauty, a splendor removed from mortality and the terrestrial. He finally encounters this beauty in the White Sybil, a strange woman-like entity thought to be "a messenger of unknown outland gods", a bringer of doom and bearer of dire prophecies. (In "The of Satampra Zeiros" she is said to have caused the desertion of Commoriom through the utterance of such a prophecy, although this is contradicted in "The Testament of Athammaus"). In appearance she is pale, lovely, insubstantial, "like an apparition descended from the moon...a creature of snow and norland light, with eyes like moon-pervaded pools". Tortha sees her fleetingly in the streets of Cerngoth, and "in that single glimpse he...found the personification of all the vague ideals and unfixed longings that had drawn him from land to land. Here was the eluding strangeness he had sought on alien breasts and waters, and beyond horizons of fire-vomiting mountains. Here was the veiled Star, whose name and luster he had never known". The effect she has on the poet makes it clear that the Sybil and the Muse of Hyperborea were one and the same conception to Smith:

> [Tortha] seemed to hear a whisper from boreal solitudes...sharp as ice-bourn air...that sang of inviolate horizons and the chill glory of lunar auroras above continents impregnable to man. ("The White Sybil")

> But at whiles her whisper comes to me, like a chill unearthly wind that...has flown over ultimate horizons of ice-bound deserts.... And hearing her far, infrequent whisper, I behold a vision of vast auroras, on continents that are wider than the world. ("The Muse of Hyperborea")

As with Valzain in "Morthylla", love had been "no more than a passing agitation of the senses" for Tortha; but after his single glimpse of the Sybil he becomes her secret worshipper. He dreams of her "such dreams as the moon might inspire in a moth...dreams through which the Sybil moved like a woman-shaped flame". (Beyond the obvious "moth and flame" motif of this passage, note the sense of distance and separation imparted by the "moon and moth" imagery: the moon is physically remote from the world of the moth, and the moth is infinitely far from comprehending the moon, and can only dream brokenly of it.) After his first glimpse of the Sybil, the everyday world becomes pale and inconsequential for Tortha, and he finds his reams of poetry "void and without meaning...like the sere leaves of a bygone year".

However, one day he sees the Sybil again, and she seems to beckon him to follow her into the high mountains. Tortha pursues her through a terrific snow storm but loses his way, and eventually passes out. He awakens in another world, like "the inmost heart of some boreal paradise...and from the bank of blossoms on which she reclined, the Sybil rose to receive her worshipper".

Tortha listens in rapture to the speech of the White Sybil, although "much was forgotten afterwards.... It was like a light too radiant to be endured". Nothing of what she tells him is directly presented to the reader, but what is hinted at bears a definite relationship to Smith's own desires and fancies:

> Something there was in her speech of time and its mystery; something of that which lies forever beyond time; something of the grey shadow of doom that waits upon world and sun; something of love, that pursues an elusive, perishing fire; of death, the soil from which all flowers spring; of life, that is a mirage on the frozen void.

This is, in short, a catalog of Smith's deepest fixations and fascinations: his poet's interest in "the ultimate, eternal Verities" of existence[81]; in doomed and dying worlds, like his creations Zothique, Mars, and Hyperborea; in the ephemerality of love; in the vampiric bond of life upon death; in the set of illusions we call reality.

So enchanted is Tortha by the speech of the Sybil that he confesses his love and seeks to embrace her.

> Dreadfully, unutterably, she seemed to change in his arms as he clasped her—to become a frozen corpse that had lain for ages in a floe-built tomb—a leper-white mummy in whose frosted eyes he read the horror of the ultimate void. Then she was a thing that had no form or name—a dark corruption that flowed and

---

81. From Smith's poem "Ode to Music" (ST).

eddied in his arms—a hueless dust, a flight of gleaming atoms...."

For all that the poet's worship is true and his heart pure, Tortha is not worthy to possess or contain the alien beauty of the Sybil. He is but a mortal human, a denizen of a far lower plane than that of the Sybil; like "the moth and the moon" they are of worlds impossibly distant.

Tortha is returned to Earth, but "ever afterward there was a cloudy dimness in his mind...like the dazzlement in eyes that have looked on some insupportable light"—he has fallen from grace, has lost a glory beyond life. In time he meets a simple maiden, Illara, whom he mistakes for the Sybil "in the darkness that had come upon him"; and Smith concludes the tale with a slight—and somewhat jarring—bit of drollery: "Illara, in her way, was content, being not the rust of mortal women whose lover had been faithful to a divine illusion".

"The Ice-Demon" (1932, AY) was the next story Smith composed after finishing "The White Sybil", and it is amusing to note that in it "the shell-shaped domes of Cerngoth [lay] deep down in the glaciation...beneath fathoms of perpetual ice". It too eschews hyperbole in its telling and is visually rich; but unlike "The White Sybil", the tale is grim rather than poetic. Quangah the huntsman and two jewellers of Iqqua mount an expedition into desolate and glacier-covered Mhu Thulan to retrieve the wealth of King Haalor, who had entered the realm fifty years before "to make war upon the polar ice". The king had sought to melt the creeping glacier with a wizard-conjured sun, but he and his party had died strangely in the attempt.

Within an ice-cavern the trio find Haalor and his men embedded in a wall of ice. After relieving the king of his jewels, they are attacked by the cavern itself, which closes upon them like a mouth. The jewellers die horribly, and Quangah flees, but the ice-fields themselves seem to trick him and hamper his flight. He eventually reaches the border of the glacier and collapses in exhaustion, but he awakens to terror:

It seemed to him that a great shadow, malign and massive and somehow *solid*, was moving upon the horizon and striding over the low hills toward the valley in which he lay. It came with inexpressible speed, and the last light appeared to fall from the heavens, chill as a reflection caught in ice.... He unslung his bow and discharged arrow after arrow, emptying his quiver at the huge and bleak and formless shadow that seemed to impend before him on the sky.... All at once the air darkened before him, with a sourceless, blue-green glimmering in its depths.... It was like phantom ice—a thing that blinded his eyes and stifled his breath, as if he were buried in some glacial tomb.

To appease the demon of the glacier Quangah rids himself of the stolen jewels, but is frozen to death nonetheless. The jewels lay beside his rigid corpse, and we are told that "in its own time, the great glacier, moving slowly and irresistibly southward, would reclaim them".

Despite its grimness, satire is not entirely absent from "The Ice Demon". Quangah first dismisses the suggestion that the advancing ice-sheet is "a great demon, cruel, greedy, and loth to give up that which it had taken"—which of course it turns out to be—because he considers such a belief only a "crude and primitive superstition, not to be entertained by enlightened minds of the Pleistocene age". Smith understood that every age *(including ours,* by implication) believes itself "enlightened", regardless of how it is seen by later eras.[82] A similar passage appears in "The Seven Geases", when, from millions of years in the past, out of a continent since fragmented and sunken, we hear tell of Ralibar Vooz's "thoroughly modem disdain of

---

82. "I'll be dammed if l can see that the present age, for all its scientific discoveries, psychoanalysis, etc., is any smarter or more sophisticated than the 18th. It is, however, equally cock-sure and materialistic—or more so.... History never does anything but plagiarize itself (letter to George Sterling, 4 November 1926).

the supernatural". It no doubt amused Smith to write of characters who suffer from what might be termed 'the *hubris* of rationality', only to subject them to strange and fantastic adventures incompatible with their narrow philosophies.

CHAPTER FOUR
AVEROIGNE

With the Averoigne[83] story-cycle, Smith came closest to producing a series with a non-fabulous backdrop. The stories that comprise the series take place in the imaginary Medieval French province of Averoigne, and the settings range in time from the twelfth century to the eighteenth.[84] But despite the firmer historical grounding, Smith had no wish to create historically accurate fiction: when called out by Lovecraft for contradicting the accepted chronology of France, Smith was unconcerned, and replied that Averoigne was "a realm no less mythical than [James Branch] Cabell's Poictesme".[85]

Averoigne is also Smith's most conventionally romantic setting, a land of dark forests and lonely castles, peopled by superstitious peasants, minstrels, and monks, with witches,

---

83. Rah Hoffman recalls that Smith pronounced this name as though it rhymed with "Kahn" (private communication).

84. The following completed stories take place in the following years: "The Maker of Gargoyles" (1138), "The Holiness of Azédarac" (1175), "The Colossus of Ylourgne" (1281), "The Beast of Averoigne" (1369), "The Mandrakes" (ca. 1400), "The Disinterment of Venus" (1550), "A Rendezvous in Averoigne" (ca.1550), "The Satyr" (ca.1575), "The End of the Story" (1789).

85. Letter to Lovecraft (#37, LL), 4 December 1933. Although attempts have been made to match Averoigne in a detailed way to the actual French province of Auvergne (see Glenn Rahman, "The History of Averoigne?", in *Crypt of Cthulhu* No. 26, [Hallowmass 1984]), it is unlikely that Smith took more than the hint of the name from Auvergne.

vampires, and werewolves lurking in the shadows. The completed works in the story-cycle are "The End of the Story", "The Satyr", "A Rendezvous in Averoigne", "The Holiness of Azédarac", "The Maker of Gargoyles", "The Colossus of Ylourgne", "The Mandrakes", "The Beast of Averoigne", "The Disinterment of Venus", "Mother of Toads", and "The Enchantress of Sylaire". Projected but unwritten tales include "The Queen of the Sabbath", "The Sorceress of Averoigne" (both SS), and "The Oracle of Sadaqua" (BB).

One of the finest stories in this series is "The Beast of Averoigne" (1932, LW), which Smith felt was among his most technically polished works.[86] Like "The Testament of Athammaus" and "The Double Shadow", it is in the form of a first-person account, meant for future ages, which tells of a horror witnessed by the narrator. Unlike the other Averoigne tales, the horror of this story is an unearthly one.

In the year of a red comet, a series of gruesome murders take place in the forests and villages of Averoigne. Animals, and later men, are found with their spines laid open and the marrow removed. One night in the woods, a young monk from the Benedictine Abbey of Perigon sees a horrible apparition:

> It moved as with the flitting of a fen-fire, and was of changeable color, being pale as a corposant, or ruddy as new-spilled blood, or green as the poisonous distillation that surrounds the moon...revealing dimly the black abomination of head and limbs that were not those of any creature wrought by God. The horror stood erect, rising to more than the height of a tall man; and it swayed like a great serpent, and its members undulated, bending like heated wax.

---

86. "I think that I have done better tales, but few that are technically superior". Letter to Derleth, 18 April 1933.

A few days later the monk falls prey to the creature and dies in the fashion of its other victims. With each murder, Theophile, the abbot of Perigon, grows paler and more agitated.

Luc le Chaudronnier, a sorcerer and the narrator of the story, is called upon to vanquish the Beast. He stations himself outside the Abbey one night; when the creature appears, he releases an ancient demon, pent within the ring once owned by the prehistoric wizard Eibon (thus is the story linked to the Hyperborean series). The demon defeats the Beast, which is revealed as Theophile, whose body had housed a demon from the comet.

Theophile's unwitting participation in the murders is suppressed, and it is said thereafter that he died at the hands of the Beast. The story ends with an effective evocation of the cosmic dread that permeates the work:

> ...they who will read this record in future ages will believe it not, saying that no demon or malign spirit could have prevailed thus upon true holiness. Indeed, it were well that none should believe the story: for thin is the veil betwixt man and the godless deep. The skies are haunted by that which it were madness to know; and strange abominations pass evermore between earth and moon and athwart the galaxies. Unnamable things have come to us in alien horror and will come again. And the evil of the stars is not as the evil of Earth.

In contrast to the tense and grim "Beast of Averoigne", "The Disinterment of Venus" (1932, GL) is ironic and humorous. It, too, takes place in the Abbey of Perigon. Three monks digging in "the Benedictine's turnip and carrot patches" unearth what they first think is a stone. They work to remove the obstruction "for the honor of the monastery and the glory of God" but find it to be an antique statue of Venus, dating from Roman days. The monks are affected strangely by its presence: the clearing away of soil from the statue's face and breasts, for instance, was "a task [they] performed with great thoroughness". That night the three go off drinking and wenching, and the other monks begin to complain of carnal desires.

One night the pious and zealous Brother Louis (who as it happens is "handsome as Adonis") goes forth to smash the image. In the morning he is found crushed beneath the fallen statue, with the arms of Venus clasped tightly about him. Try as they might, his fellow monks cannot release Venus' grip, so they bury him in the vegetable patch, along with the statue.

In "The Enchantress of Sylaire" (AY), a lover's rejection drives the young poet Anselme into hermitage. One day he comes upon a beautiful woman, Sephora, who leads him through a portal of Druidic stones and into another world. She announces herself as the enchantress of the region, called Sylaire, and makes it known that she wishes Anselme to remain as her consort. Sephora shares her domain with a black wolf; one day as Anselme is walking alone through the woods, the creature reveals itself to be Malachie, a werewolf. By eating a garlic-like root, he can throw off the wolf-shape for a while. Malachie claims that he is a former lover of Sephora, who tricked him into drinking water from a pool that causes lycanthropy. He warns Anselme that Sephora is "an ancient lamia, well-nigh immortal, who feeds on the vital fires of young men", and that her beauty is an illusion.

Confronted, Sephora denies all of this, and the love-struck Anselme believes her. Together, they plot to make Malachie's affliction permanent, by substituting water from the werewolf-pool for an antidote he has been brewing. The wolf goes mad after drinking the potion, and Anselme kills him with a sword.

Malachie had earlier given Anselme a mirror with the power to dispel illusion. By this time Anselme knows that Malachie had spoken truthfully about Sephora, but instead of using the mirror to reveal the true Sephora, he throws it out a window and takes her in his arms. Because she is "the essence of all the beauty and romance that he had ever craved", Anselme would prefer to accept her illusion of womanhood, than to dispel it.

"The Enchantress of Sylaire", which dates from around 1940, is the last of the Averoigne tales, and constitutes an unintentional remake of the first entry in the series, "The End of the Story" (1929, OST). The setting for "The End of the Story" is also the most modern one. In 1798, Christophe Morand takes shelter from a storm in the Abbey of Perigon. He is welcomed by the abbot, Hilaire, and is shown about the monastery's library. There he reads an illicit manuscript, which tells of a knight's adventures in the nearby ruined Château des Faussesflammes. Morand is strangely moved by the story and makes his own journey to the ruins. Because "The End of the Story" is a first person account, Smith generates a parallel structure which relates the story's narrative to the manuscript that Morand reads: we are given two manuscripts, two dooms, separated by centuries.

Morand descends a hidden staircase within the ruins and finds himself in a beautiful, sunlit world, "a land of classic myth, of Grecian legend". Nymphs and satyrs scamper about a temple; within it, he finds Nycea, "a woman of goddess-like beauty". She welcomes him with kind words but offers no explanations for herself or her world. Morand falls under her spell.

Hours later an agitated Hilaire appears on the scene, shouting prayers and sprinkling holy water. The beautiful world vanishes, and the abbot leads Morand to the surface. Hilaire explains that "the marble palace and all the luxury therein, were no more than a satanic delusion, a lovely bubble that arose from the dust and mold of immemorial death, of ancient corruption".

And though Morand is told that the beauty of Nycea is an illusion (as Anselme had similarly been warned in "The Enchantress of Sylaire"), that she is "a lamia, an ancient vampire", he can only think to regain her couch. "I lamented the beautiful dream of which [Hilaire] had deprived me.... I knew that whatever she was, woman or demon or serpent, there was no one in all the world who could ever arouse in me the same desire and the same delight". He resolves to return to Nycea, and so the story ends.

"The Holiness of Azédarac" (1931, LW) is one of Smith's

most well-rounded and enjoyable stories. Azédarac, Bishop of Ximes, "lives in the odor of incense and piety" but at the same time "maintains a private understanding with the Adversary". He secretly worships Satan, as well as other and more potent entities.[87] "The chief difference between myself and many other ecclesiastics", he tells his servant, "is that I serve the Devil wittingly and of my own free will, while they do the same in sanctimonious blindness".

Brother Ambrose is sent by the Archbishop to investigate rumors concerning Azédarac. He learns the truth about the Bishop and is on his way to deliver a report when he is met by Azédarac's henchman, disguised as a fellow traveller. At a roadside tavern, Ambrose is given wine laden with a potion that transports him seven-hundred years into the past. The year is now 475 A.D., and he finds himself in the company of Moriamis, a beautiful sorceress. She is glad for his company, but though Ambrose falls for her charms, he is reluctant to break his monastic vows. Moriamis patiently (and with a certain wit) explains that the centuries that separate him from his own age "should be long enough to procure the remission of any sin, no matter how often repeated".

Moriamis had once been the lover of Azédarac and had stolen some amount of the time-travel liquid from him before he left for the 12th century. After a time spent pleasantly with Moriamis, Ambrose resolves to return to his own age and make his report to the Archbishop. She gives him the stolen potion, along with a counter-draft that, should he wish to use it, will send him back to her.

Ambrose arrives at the tavern by the road but learns that the year is 1210, fifty-five years beyond his own time. His Archbishop is long dead, as is Azédarac, now St. Azédarac. He downs the second draft and finds Moriamis awaiting him; he never suspects that she doctored both potions to transport him forward and backward by 755 years rather than 700, thereby

---

87. As an in-joke with his friend Lovecraft, Smith has Azédarac also worship the gods of the Cthulhu Mythos.

guaranteeing his return.

In view of the journeys Ambrose undertakes, and the subterfuge and setbacks he encounters, Smith considered "The Holiness of Aredarac" an exceptionally "plotty" bit of storywriting for him.

A less attractive—though no less amorous or conniving—sorceress is presented in "Mother of Toads" (1937, TSS), a gruesomely erotic short tale. A huge and hideous witch living alone by a bog is known as *La Mère des Crapauds* or Mother of Toads, both for her amphibian neighbors and for her appearance. Pierre, an apothecary's apprentice on an errand to pick up some of her potions, attracts her fancy. She entices him with a cup of wine, into which she has introduced an aphrodisiac. He finds his passion kindled by her foul form: "The lumpish limbs had grown voluptuous; the pale, thick-lipped mouth enticed him with the promise of ampler kisses than other mouths could yield". Hours later he awakens in *La Mère's* bed, with her "her toad-like...pale, warty body pressed and bulged against him". Repulsed, Pierre runs from the hut, but becomes lost in a strange sudden fog. He strays into the bog and is attacked by an endless army of toads. Borne under the surface by the mass of their clinging bodies, Pierre perishes. In the original version of "Mother of Toads", his last impression is of "two enormous breasts" that were "crushed closely down upon his face", smothering him.[88]

The longest of the Averoigne tales (15,000 words) is "The Colossus of Ylourgne" (1932, GL). Nathaire is an infamous necromancer of Vyones, whose career parallels that of Namirrha from "The Dark Eidolon", which Smith composed six months later. His parentage is unknown and perhaps demonic; in his early years in Vyones, he was stoned for necromancy and lamed, and has since nurtured a hatred for the city and has plotted his

---

88. To market "Mother of Toads", Smith found it necessary to remove the most erotic passages from the original version of the story. See *The Unexpurgated Clark Ashton Smith* for the complete text.

revenge upon it. After he has disappeared from Vyones, corpses of the newly-dead or freshly-buried rise and begin a strange pilgrimage. Groups of the dead, "deaf, dumb, totally insensate... hurrying with horrible speed and sureness", pass into the forest. The mystery of this exodus is maintained for much of the story.

The young Gaspard du Nord, a former student of Nathaire, leaves Vyones to discover the reason for the flight of the dead, in which he sees the hand of his former master. At the ruined castle of Ylourgne, he finds Nathaire and the dead at work constructing a huge simulacra of the wizard, molded from the rendered flesh of the corpses. Du Nord is captured, but after a painful escape from the dungeons (which Smith describes at excessive length), he returns to warn Vyones. In the meanwhile, the Colossus, animated by the soul of Nathaire, leaves the castle and brings havoc to the countryside.

As the giant enters Vyones, du Nord hails it from the roof of the cathedral. When it bends over to investigate, the Colossus inhales a powder dispersed by the young sorcerer, and Nathaire's control is destroyed. In gentle bewilderment, the corpse-giant wanders into the hills and digs itself a grave, striving to retrieve the peace of death. In time, it is reduced to an "enormous, rook-haunted bulk" from which the wizard's voice is occasionally heard to issue in protest.

CHAPTER FIVE
ATLANTIS

Smith's story-cycle of Atlantis contains at most five stories; yet these tales and this cycle represent some of his best and most successful work. The stories themselves are more varied in type than in any other story-cycles. One is science-fiction ("A Voyage to Sfanomoë"); one is a poignant fable ("The Last Incantation"); two are horror stories ("The Death of Malygris" and "The Double Shadow"); and the fifth is a dream-tale ("A Vintage from Atlantis"). In addition to these stories, Smith also wrote one prose-poem about Atlantis, and several of his early poems make reference to it as a symbol of doom and loss.[89]

Smith's imagination centered on Poseidonis, which was, in his words, "the last isle of foundering Atlantis", the final remnant of the fabled lost continent of the Atlantic that sank in some prehistoric cataclysm. The legend of Atlantis is first found in Plato, and innumerable writers through the ages have retold its story, adding or disregarding details as fit their purposes. One of these writers, H. P. Blavatsky in *The Secret Doctrine*, added the idea that Atlantis did not sink in a single cataclysm, but in successive cataclysms, the last remnant to survive being called Poseidonis. That Blavatsky's work is the direct source of Smith's use of Poseidonis as a story-cycle setting is evidenced

---

89. Atlantis is central to the poems "Atlantis" and "Tolometh"; the prose poem is "From a Letter" and is remarkable as an invocation of the splendor of Atlantis. In addition Smith began a romantic play, "The Fugitives" (SS), set in Poseidonis.

in his letters.[90] Additionally, Blavatsky wrote of Atlantis as a nation of wicked magicians, as the birth-place of alchemy—ideas very similar to those used by Smith.

Atlantis/Poseidonis is a setting that, though rich in history and culture, is both fallen and doomed. In "A Voyage to Sfanomoë" (1930, LW), the inhabitants are fully aware that the final cataclysm, which will at last draw Poseidonis itself below the waves, is destined to happen in the present generation. The story tells of two brother-scientists, Hotar and Evidon, who toil in the building of a spacecraft, in which they hope to escape their doomed isle and to journey to the planet Sfanomoë (Venus). On the long voyage to Sfanomoë, they read the classics of Atlantean literature and argue and discuss the problems of philosophy and science. They grow old. But landing on Sfanomoë, they forget their cares and their pursuits; with the innocence of children, they explore the new world, finding flowers everywhere. Quickly though, the pollen in the air settles upon them and sprouts and grows. The brothers die with a strange joy, without pain, becoming themselves a part of the endless floral landscape. Though they die, they do so in happiness, and it is interesting that Hotar and Evidon—both ardent scientists and inventors—are portrayed so sympathetically throughout the story.

"The Last Incantation" (1929, LW) was the first production of Smith's major story-writing period, and it contains some of his best and most poetic evocations of the emotions of loss. In this story the archimage Malygris, weary in his high tower, gropes among the "shadows of memories" to recall his love for the maiden Nylissa, who died on the eve of their wedding day. After failing to receive advice from one of his familiars, a viper, Malygris summons the shade of his lost love. As her apparition stands before him, he begins to doubt in his heart that this is the same Nylissa whom he had loved so long ago:

---

90. "One can disregard the [tenets of] Theosophy, and make good use of the stuff about elder continents, etc. I got my own ideas about Hyperborea, Poseidonis, etc., from such sources, and then turned my imagination loose" (letter to Lovecraft, 1 March 1933, #32 of LL).

He could not be sure, and the growing doubt was succeeded by a leaden dismay, by a grim despondency that choked his heart as with ashes. His scrutiny became searching and exigent and cruel, and momently the phantom was less and less the perfect semblance of Nylissa.... The soul of Malygris grew sick again with age and despair and the death of his evanescent hope.

Dismissing the apparition, Malygris reproves his familiar, who provides the moral of the tale, a last bit of wisdom which Malygris had not possessed: "'It was indeed Nylissa whom you had summoned and saw... but no necromantic spell could recall for you your own lost youth or the fervent and guileless heart that loved Nylissa.... This, my master, was the thing that you had to learn.'"

"The Death of Malygris" (1933, LW) furthers the sorcerer's story. King Gadeiron summons twelve wizards to a secret council, where they discuss the possibility that Malygris is dead. The King's sorcerer, Maranapion, has spied upon Malygris with the far-seeing eye of a Cyclops and has discovered that, though his familiars attend him still, Malygris has not moved or stirred from his high throne in a year and a month: "he sits defying the worm, still undecayed and incorrupt."

Many of the sorcerers fear to move against Malygris, and some depart the council. At this point Smith gives an interlude wherein two of these men approach Malygris on their own; they enter the wizard's chamber, but a voice issuing from the corpse of Malygris lays a curse upon them. They dwindle in size and are struck down by one of the familiars, the viper of the previous story.[91] Thus, Smith foreshadows for his readers the upcoming doom of the King and his cohorts, who, meanwhile, have created a simulacrum of Malygris and have caused it to decay; through the power of sympathetic magic the same decay

---

91. This scene was illustrated by Smith for the story's original *Weird Tales* appearance; he considered this particular pen-and-ink drawing his finest rendering of a scene from his own tales.

has been brought about in the body of Malygris.

But Maranapion deems his victory incomplete until he himself looks upon the rotting face of Malygris. So he and the king and the other sorcerers proceed to the tower of the archimage, where the still form upon the throne curses them: as they had made Malygris decay, so shall they decay—but while still living, and all in the space of an hour. Smith gives a gruesome account of their ends:

> ...each was aware of his own limbs that rotted beneath him, pace by pace, and felt the quick sloughing of his flesh in corruption from the bone. Crying out with tongues that shrivelled 'ere the cry was done, they fell down on the floor of the chamber. Life lingered in them.... In the dark agony of their live corruption, they tossed feebly to and fro...till their brains were turned to gray mold, and the sinews were parted from their bones, and the marrow was dried up.

"The Double Shadow" (1932, OST) is among Smith's most carefully wrought stories, though it suffers from a wordiness and dryness of tone that recalls the excesses of the Hyperborean series. The story is a first-person narrative, the record of a young sorcerer, Pharpetron, apprentice to the great Avyctes, the sole surviving pupil of Malygris. The style of the narrative is consistent with that of a pedantic, scholarly student of the occult, but is nonetheless rather cold and unsatisfying.

Smith used a writing-technique in the story that was often employed by his friend H. P. Lovecraft: the gradual crescendo of the excitement of the story to a climax in the last sentence. The first paragraph of the story is used to set the tone for what is to follow:

> My name is Pharpetron, among those who have known me in Poseidonis; but even I, the last and most forward pupil of the wise Avyctes, know not the name

of that which I am fated to become ere to-morrow. Therefore, by the ebbing silver lamps, in my master's marble house above the loud, ever-ravening sea, I write this tale with a hasty hand, scrawling an ink of wizard-virtue on the grey, priceless, antique parchment of dragons. And having written, I shall enclose the pages in a sealed cylinder of orichalchum, and shall cast the cylinder from a high window into the sea, lest that which I am doomed to become should haply destroy the writing.... Having read my story, men will learn the truth and take warning; and no man's feet, henceforth, will approach the pale and demon haunted house of Avyctes.

Thus, at the very beginning the ending is obvious—and that the writer, with whom readers sympathize, is doomed. The narrative exists to tell us why.

Pharpetron and Avyctes have discovered a mirror-bright tablet, writ with alien ciphers. In his thirst for knowledge, Avyctes seeks the key to these ciphers, summoning up the ghosts of sorcerers from the distant past and inquiring of them. In a very effective distancing-technique, the sorcerers learn from a "dim, tenuous ghost of a sorcerer from prehistoric years", that the ciphers are those of an ancient serpent-people, who were only "a dubious legend" even in the ghost's long-lost age. Avyctes sends this ghost deeper into the past to find the meaning of the ciphers.

This writing, they learn, constitutes some kind of spell, an invocation, but with no corresponding spell of renunciation. Nevertheless, the wizard and his young assistant perform the rite, together with an animated mummy, Oigos, but nothing seems to come in answer to the summons. Many days pass, and the invocation is forgotten.

Some time later it is discovered that Avyctes is followed by a double shadow: in addition to his own shadow, there is another, one of unearthly hue and monstrous form, impervious to any spells. When it finally touches the shadow of Avyctes, the wizard becomes the unspeakable thing that cast the strange shadow. The same fate overtakes Oigos, showing that there is a power at work beyond even the laws of death. Lastly the shadow approaches Pharpetron, and he writes:

> ...the horror that was Avyctes, and the second horror that was Oigos, have left me not, and neither do they tremble. And with eyes that are not eyes, they seem to brood and watch, waiting till I too shall become as they. And their stillness is more terrible than if they had rended me limb from limb.... I have shut myself in the room of volumes and books and have written this account.... And now I must make an end, and enclose this writing in a sealed cylinder of orichalchum, and fling it forth to drift upon the wave. For the space between my shadow and the shadow of the horror is straightened momently...and the space is no wider than the thickness of a wizard's pen.

The story ends here, and the reader is left as much in the dark about the fate of the doomed as the doomed are themselves. The atmosphere of the unknown remains inviolate.

"A Vintage from Atlantis" (1931, AY) itself contains no references to Poseidonis, and indeed, were it not for Smith's own listing of it with the other Atlantean stories (under the heading "Tales of Atlantis") in his *Black Book*, one could plausibly argue for its exclusion from the story-cycle. The setting for the story is historic rather than imaginary; the action takes place during the time of pirates and the Spanish supremacy on the open seas.

Again we have a first-person narrative, but this time it is the tale of a survivor. The tale tells of the discovery in an island cove of an ancient jar of wine. Drinking the wine, the sailors see a vision of sunken Atlantis, which seems to beckon to them; and reaching out to enter the world they see, the men tread into the ocean and are drowned. One sailor escapes this fate only because he had drunk less of the wine than the others, and lives to see the vision fade away:

> "Slowly the waters darkened above the fading spires and walls; and the midnight blackened upon the sea; and [Atlantis] was lost like the vanished bubbles of wine".

CHAPTER SIX
MARS

The Martian sequence of tales is comprised by "The Vaults of Yoh-Vombis", "The Dweller in the Gulf", "Vulthoom", and the unfinished "Mnemoka". Each story is set upon Mars at a time when the planet has only begun to be explored by Man.

Like Zothique, Mars is portrayed as an aging world, slowly dying beneath "a sky...dark as the brine of desert seas that have ebbed to desert pools".[92] The semi-human native race, the Aihais, are described as tall, lean of limb and massive of chest, with "high-flaring ears and pit-like nostrils".[93] They are ancient and uncommunicative, and they add a sense of mystery and other-worldly strangeness to the series that is not found in the Zothique story-cycle:

> More deeply than in daylight, they apprehended the muffled breathings and hidden, tortuous movements of a life forever inscrutable to the children of other planets. The void between Earth and Mars had been traversed; but who could cross the evolutionary gulf between Earthman and Martian?

---

92. "The Dweller in the Gulf". One month before writing "The Vaults of Yoh-Vombis" Smith fought a brush fire that at one point threatened his cabin; it is interesting to note that for days afterward he claimed that "the sky seemed as dark and dingy as the burnt-out sky of the planet Mars" (letter to Derleth, 20 July 1931).

93. "Vulthoom".

> The people were friendly enough in their taciturn way: they had tolerated the intrusion of terrestrials, had permitted commerce between the worlds. Their languages had been mastered, their history studied, by terrene savants. But it seemed that there could be no real interchange of ideas. Their civilization had grown old in diverse complexity before the foundering of Lemuria; its sciences, arts, religions, were hoary with inconceivable age; and even the simplest customs were the fruit of alien forces and conditions.[94]

This sense of unearthliness was an important element of the series for Smith: "As far as I'm concerned...the interplanetary angle...adds considerably to the interest, particularly since the stories have little or nothing in common with the usual science fiction stuff".[95]

The use of Mars as a setting may have been the result of a writing assignment given to Smith by *Wonder Stories* magazine. In July 1931, he was commissioned to write a story around a synopsis entitled "The Martian", written by E. M. Johnston, that had won second place in the *Wonder Stories Quarterly* 'Interplanetary Plot Contest'. The completed story[96] takes terrestrial adventurers to the red planet.

The next story Smith wrote was the first Martian-series tale, "The Vaults of Yoh-Vombis", begun four weeks after "The Martian". It, too, has earthmen encountering the mysteries of Mars. That "The Martian" influenced the choice of setting for "The Vaults of Yoh-Vombis" is suggested by the details of the latter story's synopsis. Set down fairly early in his fiction-writing period—perhaps as early as 1929 on the basis of manu-

---

94. *Ibid.*

95, Letter to Derleth, 22 September 1931.

96. Smith's original title for this story was "The Martian"; *Wonder Stories* published it as "The Planet-Entity", and Smith retitled it "Seedling of Mars" for inclusion in TSS.

script evidence—the synopsis for "The Vaults of Yoh-Vombis" (then called "The Vaults of Abomi") originally set the action "on a dying world". Only at some later point did Smith change this sentence to read "in a deserted ancient city on Mars".

"The Vaults of Yoh-Vombis" (OST) is an exceptionally powerful and successful tale, although one that was substantially edited for publication.[97] It has been called "one of the most purely horrific stories that Smith ever created",[98] and "different and exciting.... A horror story set...on another world and told in the luxuriant, 'gorgeous' prose traditional to heroic fantasy".[99] In the story, a party of archaeologists is investigating the ruined Martian city of Yoh-Vombis, deserted for over forty thousand years. They are struck by the age and strangeness of the place: "The stark, eroded stones were things that might have been reared by the toil of the dead, to house the monstrous ghouls and demons of primal desolation.... [The city was] like the mausolea of primordial giants, that abide from darkness-eaten aeons to confront the last dawn of an expiring orb".[100] They descend into the underground parts of the city; and in the manner of Lovecraft's scientists in *At the Mountains of Madness*, they read

---

97. The deletions were made at the request of *Weird Tales* editor Farnsworth Wright, who wanted Smith "to speed up the first part...by cutting out two or three thousand words of carefully built atmospheric preparation" (letter from Smith to Derleth, 23 October 1931). In the end, however, the total deletion amounted to about 1500 words. At the time Smith pledged to "restore most of it, if the tale is ever brought out in book form" (letter to Lovecraft, ca. early November 1931, #25, LL), but for some reason he never did. See *The Unexpurgated Clark Ashton Smith* for the complete text.

98. Donald Sidney-Fryer, "The Last Enchanter", introduction to *The Last Incantation* (NY: Pocket/Timescape Books, 1982).

99. Lin Carter, "Other Stars and Skies", *Xiccarph* (New York: Ballantine, 1972). Carter also notes the similarity between the early work of C. L. Moore, particularly her "Northwest Smith" stories, and Smith's Martian series tales, which precede them.

100. This excerpt belongs to the material cut by Smith prior to publication in *Weird Tales*.

of the last days of Yoh-Vombis from its painted walls.[101] In the deepest vault a musty, mat-like creature drops upon the head of their leader, Allan Octave. Thereafter, he acts as if possessed, and strives to open a certain bricked-up door. The narrator, Rodney Severn, slashes the bloated creature upon Octave's head:

> The knife tore into it as if through rotten parchment, making a long gash, and the horror appeared to collapse like a broken bladder. Out of it there gushed a sickening torrent of human blood, mingled with dark, filiated masses that may have been half-dissolved hair, and floating gelatinous lumps like molten bone, and shreds of a curdy white substance.

From the now-open door comes a flood of these leech-like monsters, "creatures of ultramundane night and cycle-sealed corruption". (We note another distinctively Lovecraftian phrase: some of these creatures "crawled with glutted slowness.... What they had found to feed on in the sealed eternal midnight I do not know; and I pray that I shall never know".) The remaining men fleet but Severn alone makes it to the surface, after fighting off an attack by one of the creatures. He is brought to a Martian hospital but later is overcome by a weird compulsion to return to the Vaults, apparently instilled in him by his contact with the leech. Severn breaks his bonds and escapes; presumably, he returns to Yoh-Vombis.

The second Martian story, "The Dweller in the Gulf" (1932, AY), was composed about a year later. Three fortune-hunters, seeking shelter from a desert storm, find a cavern that leads into the Martian underworld. A path winds down to a subterranean lake, the last remnant of a Martian sea.[102] The three are

---

101. In fact, Smith read *At the Mountains of Madness* one month before writing "The Vaults of Yoh-Vombis". It seems likely that Smith's use of wall-paintings was inspired by Lovecraft's short novel.

102. A similar notion is presented in Smith's poem in prose "Sadastor"

captured by a group of eyeless Martians, a degenerate offshoot of the Yorhis, the race that had built Yoh-Vombis. They are brought to a blinded earthman, John Chalmers, who tells them that the Yorhis worship a strange creature that lives in the lake. He shows them a metallic sculpture of the thing, which when rubbed induces a drug-like state of delirium. The earthmen participate in a religious ceremony, and Chalmers instructs them to touch the image:

> "Do as I am doing...and you won't mind the darkness so much. You don't miss your eyes or need them here. You'll drink the putrid water of the lake, you'll eat the raw slugs, the raw blind fish and lake-worms, and find them good.... And you won't know if the Dweller comes and gets you".
>
> Even as he spoke he began to caress the image, running his hands over the gibbous carapace, the flat reptilian head. His blind face took on the dreamy langour of an opium-eater, his voice died to inarticulate murmurs, like the lapping sound of a thick liquid.

When all have been rendered unconscious by the action of the drug, the Dweller rises up to feed; later, the half-eaten body of Chalmers is found near the altar, beside a trail of wet prints leading to the lake. Like the typical characters of Lovecraft's stories, the three adventurers fail to understand the implications of the scene before them. Still, they try to escape the underworld but find The Dweller waiting for them on the path. Each man in turn has his eyes plucked out by the creature, and all are led back into the depths.

Smith described the first version of this tale, entitled "The Eidolon of the Blind", as "a first-rate interplanetary horror, sans the hokum of pseudo-explanation".[103] This draft was rejected

---

(OST, PP).

103. Letter to Derleth, 20 September 1932. For the text of the original

by *Weird Tales* (it was considered too terrible and horrific), and *Wonder Stories* would publish it only if Smith "gave the yarn more 'scientific motivation'".[104] To satisfy this demand, Smith felt forced to write-in the character of Chalmers to provide just such a "pseudo-explanation" for the story's events. And to add insult to injury, Hugo Gernsback ordered the *Wonder Stories* editor to remove several paragraphs of atmospheric description, and to rewrite the story's bleak ending, which Smith had called "magnificent...Dantesque".[105] As noted above, in Smith's own ending—and as it reads in subsequent book publications—all three earth adventurers are captured and blinded by The Dweller. In the magazine appearance this was changed to permit one character to escape, after witnessing the fate of his companions. So incensed was Smith by this tampering that he mailed off copies of the unadulterated conclusion to a large number of his correspondents, and effectively wrote nothing more for *Wonder Stories*.

The more fortunate—though less successful—"Vulthoom" (1932-33, GL) also deals with horrors lurking beneath the surface of Mars. Two Earthmen in Ignarh, the principal city of Mars, are summoned to the cave-world of Ravormos by Vulthoom, the Devil of Martian legendary. Recently awakened from a thousand-year hibernation, Vulthoom reveals that he is an alien space-traveller who arrived on Mars aeons ago.[106] He is wearying of this dying world, wishes to migrate to Earth, and proposes that the two terrestrials become his acolytes. They refuse, and after undergoing diverse adventures, one of the pair smashes a vial containing a sleep-gas that induces the aeon-long

---

version, see *The Unexpurgated Smith*.

104. Letter from Smith to Derleth, 15 November 1932. This was a common complaint of Smith's editors, and is discussed later in the chapter on "Science Fantasies".

105. Letter to Derleth, 20 September 1932.

106. On the basis of Vulthoom's statement, that he is an "intercosmic exile, banished by implacable foes", Lin Carter suggests that Vulthoom be added to the pantheon of the Lovecraftian Cthulhu Mythos.

hibernation in Vulthoom and his subjects, and in them as well.

In typical Smith fashion, the Earthmen are told all about the sleep-gas vials, both their function and their whereabouts, during a tour of the cavern; the story's climax comes about with no gyrations or complications of plot. But Vulthoom's defeat is only a temporary one, for after a thousand years, he and his followers will awaken and the plans for the conquest of Earth will be resumed. He tells the two men, who are themselves doomed never to awaken from the long sleep, "you, who dared to interfere, will lie beside me then as a little dust...and the dust will be swept away".

The unfinished "Mnemoka" (SS) tells the tale of Space-Alley Jon, a brutal drifter of the space lanes. On the basis of its extant fragments, it is clear that the thematic content of this story would have resembled that of "The Last Incantation" and "The Chain of Aforgomon", in which characters seek to recall their lost loves from the past. Jon purchases an illicit drug called *mnemoka* that allows memories to be re-lived with the strength of real experiences; he seeks to resurrect the memory of his first youthful amorous episode with the lovely Sophia. However, he is warned that "sometimes the re-lived events...take a variant turn, with intervals or endings not hitherto experienced. Such variations, it would seem, are determined by hidden desires—or fears". As Jon is walking through an alley-way in Ignarh, the drug begins to take effect:

> The barb-tipped cold had become a little blunted, as if a premature sun had risen somewhere behind the lofty maze of buildings. In lieu of the metal-hard pavement, he seemed to be treading at times on something resilient as grass or moss. The familiar alley-stenches no longer stung his nostrils with ammoniac keenness; and through them he caught evanescent waftures of bruised mint—faint but at moments unmistakable.... There was no mint anywhere on Mars. But he had lain long ago—and not alone—in a bed of mint on his natal

Earth. It was that episode, removed in time by years spent on half the solar worlds, which he wished to re-experience.

Jon's mind wanders, and he thinks of a group of jewels he had recently stolen. Suddenly he stumbles over the corpse of a former accomplice, whom he had killed for those jewels on a space-flight from Europa to Mars. As the effect of the drug grows stronger, Jon believes alternately that he is with Sophia on Earth, and aboard the space-flyer *Pelican*, disposing of his partner's body. Here the extant story ends, but it is clear that whatever dark fate Smith had in mind for Space-Alley Jon revolved around the warning that the resummoned memories "may take a variant turn", possibly involving some synthesis of his memories of Sophia and the murder of his accomplice.

CHAPTER SEVEN
OTHER WEIRD FICTION AND HORRORS

Roughly one-third of Clark Ashton Smith's short stories can be classified as weird or horror fiction not belonging to any story-cycle.

The goal of these weird stories, like Smith's works in other areas, was the liberation of imagination and the creation of a dark and exotic beauty. This he accomplished most readily in tales with a fantastic, extraterrestrial, or historically-distant setting; however, under Lovecraft's influence Smith also composed modern horror stories, in which the generation and maintenance of atmosphere is paramount, but in which the imaginative aspects are confined to a single supernatural character or event. Although Smith admitted that he found modern settings for his stories "rather uncongenial",[107] such stories were more easily marketable than his poetic fantasies or name-only "science fictions".

The tales of horror which utilize a contemporary setting are by their nature among Smith's most conventional productions, and as a result, they show the greatest influence of other writers. He acknowledged that several tales were directly inspired by well-known works: Arthur Machen's "The Great God Pan" provided the germinal seed for "The Nameless Offspring", Lovecraft's "The Statement of Randolph Carter" brought about "The Epiphany of Death" (which after Lovecraft's death Smith

---

107. Letter to Derleth, 28 August 1930.

dedicated to him), while "Pickman's Model", also by Lovecraft, begat "The Hunters from Beyond".[108]

"Genius Loci" (1932, GL) stands out as Smith's most chilling, understated, and effective venture in the genre or sub-genre of the horror story. The painter Francis Amberville is visiting the California ranch of a writer-friend, Murray. His artistic fancy is attracted by a lonely, stagnant pond, ringed by "sickly-looking alders which seem to fling themselves backwards, as if unwilling to approach it". Although he feels it to be a place of vague evil ("It is silent and desolate...it is unholy in a way I simply can't describe"), Amberville resolves to travel there daily to sketch or paint the scene. At times he sees the apparition of an old man who fits the description of Chapman, a man found dead beside the tarn years before.

As the days wear on, Amberville grows surly, secretive, compulsive. The writer's suspicions become aroused by this uncharacteristic behavior and he makes his own journey to the pool, where he finds Amberville almost hypnotized before his canvas. Murray himself is not immune to the atmosphere of the place: "That infamous, eerie scene depressed me beyond measure. It seemed that the boggy bottom was trying to drag me down in some intangible way. The boughs of the sick alders beckoned. The pool, over which the bony willow presided like an arboreal death, was wooing me foully with its stagnant waters". Amberville becomes more indrawn after this; one night, Murray realizes the full depth of his friend's strange possession: "Beside me, in the lamplit room, behind the mask of his humanity, a thing that was not wholly human seemed to sit and wait". In desperation, he arranges for Amberville's fiancée, Avis Olcott, to visit the ranch, but she proves too weak-willed to turn him from the lure of the pool.

In the end, Murray finds both Amberville and the woman dead in the tarn. Floating above their bodies he fleetingly sees

---

108. For a further discussion of the literary interplay between Lovecraft and Smith, see "CAS & Divers Hands: Ideas of Lovecraft and Others in Smith's Fiction", in Part II of this book.

"a malign, luminous, pallid emanation...a phantom projection of the pale and deathlike willow, the dying alders, the reeds, the stagnant pool and its suicidal victims":

> The landscape was visible through it, as through a film; but it seemed to curdle and thicken gradually in places, with some unholy, terrifying activity. Out of these curdlings, as if disgorged by the ambient exhalation, I saw the emergence of three human faces that partook of the same nebulous matter, neither mist nor plasma. One of these faces seemed to detach itself from the bole of a ghostly willow; the second and third swirled upward from the seething of the phantom pool, with their bodies trailing formlessly among the tenuous boughs. The faces were those of old Chapman, Francis Amberville, and Avis Olcott.

After the fashion of his best science fiction stories, such as "The City of the Singing Flame" and "The Light from Beyond", "Genius Loci" retains an air of undispelled mystery and the unknown. Murray confesses this at the end, saying that nothing he could add to the narrative "would lessen the abominable mystery of it all in any degree". And again like "The City of the Singing Flame", the narrator knows he shall be drawn back to the place of doom and shall suffer the fate of his companions.

Other horror tales by Smith are less successful. His techniques and inclinations were ill-suited to anything that partook of the contemporary, the realistic—conventional horrors succeed through an air of verisimilitude, an atmosphere of broken or interrupted realism, that Smith was either unable or unwilling to supply to his own modern stories.

One of the best-known horrors, "The Return of the Sorcerer" (1931, OST, dramatized by the *Night Gallery* television series in the early 1970's), is an example of Smith's melodramatic and ham-fisted approach to the generation of spectral atmosphere. A young man accepts the post of secretary to a recluse. He feels sourceless premonitions of doom; he meets his employer in a room "whose musty shadows could never have been wholly dissipated by sun or lamplight"; he is told that the recluse's brother "has gone away on a long trip"—but of course, the brother has actually been done away with.

The secretary is asked to read a passage from the *Necronomicon*, Lovecraft's invented book of dread secrets, which states that even a *dismembered* wizard can rise up from death to seek vengeance. Smith gives it all away with this quotation, and there is no surprise when we later learn that the old man had chopped his brother into little bits, and is now being haunted in a piecemeal fashion. While this technique of slap-in-the-face foreshadowing succeeds in the fantasy world of Zothique—in "The Tomb-Spawn", say, when the story-teller details the horrors that the main characters are doomed to encounter—it eviscerates "The Return of the Sorcerer". And Smith was imitating Lovecraft at his worst with such lines as, "horror-breeding hints and noisome intuitions invaded my brain".

Similarly, "The Treader of the Dust" (1935, LW) suffers from heavy-handed treatment and cliché characters, but is redeemed by some exquisite ideas and images. The studious main character, Sebastian, a dabbler in the occult and the recipient of an "old mansion together with a generous income", inadvertently summons up Quachil Uttaus, The Treader of the Dust. This ultra-terrestrial demon brings the decay of ages at his touch. As a result, Sebastian's study is a mass of dust and rotting furniture, and his man servant has been reduced to a mound of powder. Old age descends in seconds upon the occultist, but before his death, he witnesses the return of Quachil Uttaus:

> His eyes, lifting with enormous effort, saw for the first time that a rough, irregular gap had appeared in the room's outer wall.... Through it a single star shone into the chamber, cold and remote as the eye of a demon glaring across intercosmic space.

Out of that star—or from the spaces beyond it—a beam of livid radiance, wan and deathly, was hurled like a spear upon Sebastian....

He was as one petrified by the gaze of the Gorgon. Then, through the aperture of ruin, there came something that glided stiffly and rapidly into the room toward him, along the beam. The wall seemed to crumble, the rift widened as it entered.

It was a figure no larger than a young child, but sere and shriveled as some millennial mummy. Its hairless head, its unfeatured face, borne on a neck of skeleton thinness, were lined with a thousand reticulated wrinkles. The body was like that of some monstrous, withered abortion that had never drawn breath.... Upright and rigid, the horror floated swiftly down the wan, deathly gray beam toward Sebastian.

"The Demon of the Flower" (1931, LW) is one of Smith's few entirely extraterrestrial fantasies, and is the short story extension of his prose-poem "The Flower-Devil" (ca. 1920) with plot elements taken from his poem "The Hashish-Eater" (1920). The prose-poem describes the animate, serpentine vegetation of Saturn, ruled by a single monstrous blossom, while one of the episodes of "The Hashish Eater"—now famous because of this short story—reads,

> ...In Some Antarean world I see
> The sacred flower with lips of purple flesh,
> And silver-lashed, vermillion-lidded eyes
> Of torpid azure; whom his furtive priests
> At moonless eve in terror seek to slay
> With bubbling grails of sacrificial blood
> That hide a hueless poison....

Betraying its origins in an imagistic prose-poem, "The Demon of the Flower" leads off with eight full paragraphs of lush description, depicting life on the planet Lophai where people play a subordinate role to the vicious, semi-intelligent plants. The plants are themselves subordinate to the Voorqual, an ancient spirit living within a huge blossom-bearing tree. A priesthood worships the Voorqual, and once a year one of their number is sacrificed to the malign plant. When Nala, the betrothed of King Lunithi, is chosen for sacrifice,[109] the king nurtures a secret plan to destroy the Demon of the Flower.

This incident introduces a plot-line to the story, but the role of 'plot' is underplayed from the start. We immediately suspect that the king's plan will fail, for he is introduced as "the last if not the first of his race" to rebel against the Voorqual. And as in "The Empire of the Necromancers", Smith conveniently provides a weapon to fight an unassailable tyranny, in this case a *deus ex machina* in the form of a second ancient demon: "Lunithi remembered an old myth about the existence of a neutral and independent being known as the Occlith: a demon coeval with the Voorqual". Typical of Smith, however, the shortcomings of the Occlith as a plot-device are offset by the creativity of its conception. In contrast to the botanical Voorqual, the Occlith rules a fabulous realm of arid stone, gorgeous mineral outcroppings, and lethal chemical pools. In appearance, the Occlith has "the likeness of a high cruciform pillar of blue mineral, shining with its own esoteric luster"; the oracle it delivers is in a voice "like the tinkling of mineral fragments lightly clashed together".

Lunithi is told to poison the grail of sacrificial blood offered up yearly to the Voorqual. This he does, using a layer of his own blood to hide the "hueless poison", and the hoary plant crumbles before his eyes. But Nala, whom he has saved from sacrifice, becomes the next host for the Voorqual, and Lunithi watches as her fair form assumes the horrible lineaments of the devil-plant. The tale ends with words of unrelinquished doom, both personal and worldy: "He knew then that the Voorqual had

---

109. The scene in which Nala is selected by the Voorqual is echoed in "The Immortals of Mercury", composed three months after "The Demon of the Flower".

returned to claim its sacrifice and to preside forever above the city Lospar and the world Lophai".

In "A Tale of Sir John Maundeville" (1930; OD) and "The Ghoul" (1930; OD), Smith employs antique settings to provide breathing-room for his imagination and to distance his readers from the mundane. In the latter tale, set in Arabia at the time of Vathek, a sorrow-stricken young man agrees to an abominable pact: he will supply a ghoul with eight fresh corpses, killed by his own hand, to insure that his dead wife's body will be left undefiled. After the death of the seventh victim, he is arrested and brought to trial but is released after the circumstances of the affair become known. The judge is certain that the young man "will render justice to himself and to all others concerned"; this he does, by killing himself and becoming the eighth and final meal for the ghoul.

"A Tale of Sir John Maundeville" carries on the adventures of the fourteenth-century journeyman as chronicled in *The Voyages and Travels of Sir John Maundeville* (or *Mandeville*). Sir John enters a barren desert given over wholly to Death, ruled by a monstrous charnel worm, king of the realm "by virtue of having conquered and devoured the mortal ruler thereof, as well as those who were his subjects". For entering this land of the dead, Sir John is punished with imprisonment in a tomb, that he might learn "the things which none should behold with living eyes". He lives for days in the putrid darkness, with rotting cadavers for his companions. When he is set free, Sir John makes haste to more hospitable lands.

"The Chain of Aforgomon" (1933-34, OST) returns to the favorite theme of loss, and represents one of Smith's most substantial fantasies. John Milwarp, a writer of exotic Oriental novels, has died under mysterious circumstances; moreover, the memory of his very existence has begun to fade from the minds of his friends and readers, and even the ink in his diary is fast fading into illegibility. This document reveals that Milwarp had felt all his life a sense of distant longing, "a sentiment of formless, melancholy desire for some nameless beauty long perished out of time". Seeking the source of this half-recalled loss, Milwarp experiments with a drug which has the power to transport the soul into its previous incarnations. He travels backward in time in this fashion and, upon awakening, discovers that he is Calaspa, a citizen of the planet Hestan, a world that predates the formation of the Earth. There he is a priest of the time-god Aforgomon; but he is also in mourning over the death of his lover, Belthoris. It was the echo of this loss that had plagued the contemporary Milwarp: "Sorrow and desolation choked my heart as ashes fill some urn consecrated to the dead; and all the hues and perfumes of the garden about me were redolent only of the bitterness of death". In the blackness of his anger and despair, Calaspa repudiates Aforgomon and calls upon a rival god—handy things to have around, these rival gods—to restore one single hour of his life with Belthoris. The request is granted, but his brief happiness is tarnished by a lover's spat that takes place just as the hour ends. He feels that "vain... like all other hours, was the resummoned hour; and doubly irredeemable was my loss".

For defying "the sacred logic of time", his fellow priests condemn him to death, after decreeing that, in some incarnation ages hence, he shall remember his crime against Aforgomon and die again. This is the doom that befell Milwarp. Even his place in Time has been taken away, and all memory of him is swiftly being erased; soon it will be as if he had never lived.

The story begins with a contemporary setting but moves on to a realm distant in both time and space, and this second setting is by far the more successful. Smith spends little time with the life of the terrestrial Milwarp, and the mental journey backward to Hestan is rushed, perfunctory, and unconvincing ("The walls of Nineveh, the columns and towers of unnamed cities rose before me and were swept away. I saw the luxuriant plains that are now the Gobi desert. The sea-lost capitals of Atlantis were drawn to light in unquenched glory"). One senses that Smith wished to put the modern portion of the tale behind him as quickly as possible, at the expense of believability. Once on Hestan, the story adopts fully the poetic and emotional tone of Smith's best fantasies.

"The Devotee of Evil" (1930, AY) is a variation on the classic theme of the Medusa, a myth of long-standing interest to Smith. Set in Auburn, the tale involves the invocation of pure evil. Philip Hastane, fiction writer and narrator of the story, is approached by Jean Averaud, a mysterious newcomer. This meeting provides an example of one-line characterization, in addition to more heavy-handed foreshadowing: Hastane "was struck... by the fiery fixity of Averaud's gaze—the gaze of a man who is dominated by one idea to the exclusion of all else. Some medieval alchemist, who believed himself to be on the point of attaining his objective after years of unrelenting research, might have looked as he did". Averaud has the theory that evil is a physical phenomena, "a sort of dark vibration, the radiation of a black sun",[110] inadvertently focused by certain material objects, thus giving rise to haunted houses, cursed jewels, and the like. He has invented a device, a contraption of mirrors and bells, that will perfectly focus this radiation. Averaud succeeds in the end but is petrified into a sable statue by the evil light. As with nearly all of Smith's stories, the prose of "The Devotee of Evil" is technically polished, but the ornate phraseology and overuse of metaphor jars with the commonplace modern surroundings.

"The Nameless Offspring" (1931, AY) reaches the pinnacle of gruesome horror in Smith's fiction, and despite its conventional characters, setting, and devices, the story remains gripping and effective. The tale leads off with a remarkable "quotation" from the *Necronomicon* (written by Smith); and like Lovecraft's tales, the first paragraph of the text tells of the devastating effect the strange experiences have had on the narrator: "the broken reflex of its horrors has crowded out in perspective the main events of normal life; has made them seem no more than frail gossamers,

---

110. This notion anticipates Smith's unfinished novella "The Infernal Star" (1933, SS), in which a character travels to Yamil Zacra and Yuzh, a pair of suns, one white and one black, that disseminate pure evil through their light.

woven on the dark, windy verge of some unsealed abyss". A traveller, Chaldane, is overtaken by a storm and seeks shelter in a mansion, which by coincidence is the home of a school-chum of his father. Conveniently for the story, he has heard of the shadowy history of the Tremoth household: thirty years ago, the Lady Tremoth had been certified dead and placed within the family vaults, but awoke from her cataleptic state the next day and told of "a pale, hideous, unhuman face" that was leaning above her when she came to. Nine months later, she gave birth and died; the child was shut away.

Sir John Tremoth, aging and infirm, greets Chaldane in a manner "impeccably courteous and even gracious. But the voice was that of one to whom the ordinary relations and actions of life had long since become meaningless and perfunctory". On their way to the guest bedroom, they pass the bolted door of the room containing Tremoth's still-living 'son', a room which adjoins the master suite. That night Sir John dies; on the following night, his body awaits burial, and Chaldane and the manservant are keeping vigil. A hideous scratching and mewling begins in the next room, and in time the inhabitant therein breaks through the wall. Both men are knocked unconscious and upon recovering find that Sir John's corpse has been half-devoured. Horribly-shapen tracks lead back to the nighted vaults.

In sharp contrast to a tale like "The Nameless Offspring", Smith's later (post 1930s) weird stories and horrors frequently incorporate elements of humor and satire. In "Schizoid Creator" (1952, TSS)—an otherwise undistinguished and choppily-written piece—Smith postulates a schizophrenic God, a dual entity manifesting alternately the aspects of the Creator and the Devil. In essence Smith is saying, cynically, that with the world as it is, God must be crazy. A psychiatrist summons up a minor demon from Hell, whom he mistakes for the Devil, and subjects it to electro-shock therapy in hopes of affecting a cure. The demon is unhurt, but also unamused, by this treatment. It smashes the laboratory and departs; the psychiatrist is left a babbling madman and is committed to an asylum by his colleagues. The demon returns to Hell and informs the Adversary of its experiences, and is instructed to keep the psychiatrist well-bewildered for the remainder of his days. Afterwards, leaving Hell by a little-known door, the Devil, transformed into the Creator, makes his way into Heaven.

The posthumously published "Strange Shadows" (1940-41, SS)[111] engages in some satire of particular relevance to Smith. The main character, Gaylord Jones, is deliberate self-parody—"Gaylord" was the maiden name of Smith's mother, thus "Gaylord Jones" is a play on "Ashton Smith". The story details some unusual effects of the excessive consumption of alcohol, a subject of some concern for Smith in the late 1930s and early 1940s. The style of this story was probably tailored for *Unknown Worlds* magazine; certainly the short, clipped sentences, the paucity of metaphor and uncommon words, along with a heavy use of slang, separate "Strange Shadows" from Smith's other writings. The tale's beginning illustrates some of these differences:

> Downing his thirteenth dry martini, Gaylord Jones drew a complacent sigh and regarded the barroom floor with grave attention. He was drunk. He knew that he was drunk. With superb lucidity, he calculated the exact degree of his inebriation.
>
> A great white light was pivoted in his brain. He could turn this light, instantly, on the most obscure corners of the nothingness called life. At last he was able to appreciate the absurd logic of the cosmos. It was all very simple. Nothing mattered in the least.
>
> It was all very simple, and nothing mattered as long as one could keep himself sufficiently pickled. Ah, that was the problem. Reflecting long and deeply,

---

111. Three versions of "Strange Shadows" have come down to us, the last of which is fragmentary. I refer to the middle version, also published in *Year's Best Fantasy Stories: 1985*, ed. Arthur Saha (New York: DAW, 1985).

Jones decided that just one more martini would help to maintain his intoxication at the right stage.

On the way to the fourteenth martini, Jones stumbles over his own shadow, which has the appearance of a goatish satyr. The shadows of other people are equally "cock-eyed" and mock their owners: "A rich and popular society matron was paired with the four-legged shadow of a humpbacked cow. Shadows like those of hogs and hyenas trotted behind respectable bankers and aldermen". Jones' overindulgence in alcohol had somehow given him a distorted view of the astral plane, in which the true natures of individuals are reflected in the shadows they cast.

In the course of the story, Jones loses his fiancée, his business partner, his secretary, and nearly his sanity; however, these semi-humorous adventures, though foretold by various shadow-happenings, are in fact prosaic enough for a *Reader's Digest* serial. We recognize Smith's hand at the end, though, when Gaylord Jones resolves—as Ashton Smith must have resolved on more than one bleak occasion—to "gather enough drinks to dissolve the very substance of reality into a shadow".

CHAPTER EIGHT
SCIENCE FANTASIES

The largest market for imaginative fiction in the 1930s was to be found in science-fiction magazines. *Amazing Stories, Wonder Stories*, and *Astounding Stories* competed on a monthly basis for works in this new genre, then commonly called "scientifiction" or "stf". Smith's desire to enter this market was a natural one: beyond purely financial considerations, his early poems had demonstrated his romantic interest in unearthly and extraterrestrial realms and flights through space,[112] and several of the prose poems that pre-date his story writing period actually take place on other worlds.

The editors of these magazines were not looking for richly colorful prose poems, however, and were more eager to recruit physicists to their pages than poets. Their interest lay in stories that extrapolated science and technology into the future and that featured the interplay of stock characters against quasi-realistic surroundings; the emphasis was on fast-paced action and adventure, a clear and straight-forward style of writing, and

---

112. Sidney-Fryer has long emphasized the continuity of Smith's artistic output. In particular he has written: "Through all three [of Smith's early poetry] collections runs the theme of what may be called the cosmic-astronomic—this theme was undoubtedly suggested to Smith by the example of the poems of a similar nature by George Sterling.... When Smith came to write in the 1930's what may nominally be termed science fiction... he was merely utilizing material he had handled fifteen to twenty years earlier". ("The Alleged Influence of Lord Dunsany on Clark Ashton Smith"; see Sec. Bib.)

simple diction. Smith reacted strongly to these editorial requirements or preferences, and each had its influence on the science fiction he would write.

Smith viewed the demand for science and machinery as further evidence of the tyranny of realism in literature and the general trend from romanticism to materialism. He also felt that it indicated an uncritical adoption of scientific reasoning as the only viewpoint for approaching the world. Smith had no great love for science, and he resented the popular belief that the scientific dogma of the day had explained—or could explain—everything in the universe, that every imaginable event could be understood solely "in terms of the test-tube".[113] He railed against the "laboratory-minded donkeys... who are so hell-bent on realism and scientific verisimilitude", and advised them to "stick to the *Scientific American* in which they will find no superstitions other than those of current materialism".[114] Smith attributed his viewpoints to an "innate romanticism that makes me at least hopeful that the Jeans and Einsteins have overlooked something",[115] as well as to a genuine skepticism of the grand claims of researchers and other pundits. "Tomorrow", he wrote, "the accepted theories of science and human psychology may be superseded by a brand new lot";[116] "the *mythology of science* [my emphasis] is not one that intrigues me very deeply".[117]

Smith defended the role of mystery and the fundamentally unknowable in science fiction in several short essays, published in the letters-columns of the "stf" magazines. He argued for the acceptance of tales that "induce a sense of cosmic mystery, terror, beauty, strangeness or sublimity"[118] without supplying pseudo-scientific explanations for their fantastic elements:

---

113. "Where Fantasy Meets Science Fiction" (PD).
114. Letter to Barlow, 16 November 1933.
115. Letter to Lovecraft (#36, LL), ca. early November 1933.
116. "Realism and Fantasy" (PD).
117. Letter to Lovecraft (#14, LL), ca. 21 October 1930.
118. Letter to Derleth, 3 November 1931.

> I think those who condemn such stories are suffering from a rather amusing—and pathetic—sort of unconscious hypocrisy.... Some of them are afraid to accept and enjoy anything—even a fairy tale—that is not couched in the diction of modern materialistic science.... They would like and praise the very stories that they condemn if the writer had used a different terminology, and had offered explanations that were even superficially logical according to known laws.[119]

Such stories, Smith contended, would naturally emphasize "ultrahuman events, forces, and scenes, which properly dwarf the terrene actors to insignificance".[120]

---

119. "Where Fantasy Meets Science Fiction" (PD).

120. Fantasy and Human Experience" (PD). This belief echoes Lovecraft's dictum that "the true hero of a marvel tale is not any human being, but simply a set of phenomena" ("Some Notes on Interplanetary Fiction"). It is interesting to note that while Lovecraft considered his statement as advancing the cause of realism in literature, Smith's own statement was a reaction against the realist school. In fact, both men were fundamentally in agreement with one another. Both considered the generation of atmosphere the most important job for a writer of imaginative fiction. For Lovecraft, the height of a weird story came when a single unnatural event was revealed against a meticulously constructed realistic background of people and places. He was interested in an atmosphere of abnormality, created through contrasts of the prosaic and the impossible; "realism" was crucial in developing the sense of normalcy against which the impossible is portrayed. On the other hand, Smith's own interests centered on descriptions of the wondrous or unnatural events themselves, on the creation of an atmosphere of awe and mystery. Fritz Leiber has noted this: "[Smith] seldom put realistic details into his stories simply for the sake of making the fantastic events more plausible, though describing such fantastic events with the greatest possible realism" ("Clark Ashton Smith: An Appreciation", IM).

Smith and Lovecraft disagreed only on the question of emphasis, on the balance of the mundane and the fantastic in their stories, and both employed detailed, "realistic" descriptions to create atmosphere and mood. But, because the moods they wished to generate were different, Lovecraft chose to emphasize and describe the mundane or realistic aspects of his stories, whereas Smith concentrated on the fantastic.

Smith's twenty or thirty science fiction tales can be grouped into three broad categories that grew out of the interaction of his attitudes with the demands of his editors. In one group of stories, Smith adheres to his stated principles; in another, he satirizes the genre; in the third group, he follows more conventional patterns.

Stories in the first category include "The City of the Singing Flame", "The Light from Beyond", "A Star-Change", "A Voyage to Sfanomoë", "Master of the Asteroid", "The Vaults of Yoh-Vombis", and "The Eternal World". These stories are rich in imagination and idea, slow on action, simple in plot, and feature strong elements of wonder and mystery. Alien characters, when such are present, are silent and unfathomable, and no real communication with Mankind is possible; they are present merely to emphasize the strangeness of distant worlds.

When Smith offered explanations for the central wonders of these stories, they were indeed only "superficially logical", and the science involved was either minimal or nonexistent. In fact, of the Smith tales accepted by the "stf" magazines, the finest were slipped past the editors through the kind of "terminology changes" he advocated above. When a character is suddenly precipitated into an unearthly realm of magic and wonder, he is said to have undergone "a process of atomic re-vibration", for example.

The second group of science-fiction stories carries this process of duping his editors and readers one step further. At times the temptation to poke fun at the genre and its restrictions became too much for Smith to resist, and he indulged in satire. "The Monster of the Prophecy", "The Letter from Mohaun Los", "The Metamorphosis of the Earth", and to some extent the *Alcyone* series, are examples of this kind of story. The "outrageous space-annihilator"[121] of "The Monster of the Prophecy" is a jab at gadgetry and pseudo-science, and the character Roger Lapham in "The Metamorphosis of the Earth" parodies the

---

121. Letter to Derleth, 3 November 1931.

omnipresent, omniscient scientist. "The Letter from Mohaun Los" satirizes blasé adventurers: when Domitian Malgraff tells his Chinese factotum that he has invented a space-flyer (here Smith makes fun of 'the boy inventor') which will whisk them both into space that night, Li Wong replies, "Me go pack.... You want plentee shirt?"

Smith was certain that much of his satire was not fully appreciated, and in a sense he was grateful for the obtuseness of his readers: "I don't think Gernsback [of *Wonder Stories*] would print my work, if he realized the Swiftian irony of some of it".[122]

Smith's third category of science fiction represents concessions to the demands of his editors. Such stories include "The Immortals of Mercury", "The Invisible City", "The Dimension of Chance", and "An Adventure in Futurity". Smith acknowledged that some of these pieces bordered on hackwork, that many were slanted for a quick sale to a particular editor ("An Adventure in Futurity", "The Dimension of Chance", and "Seedling of Mars" were actually written to order). Much less space is devoted to the creation of place and atmosphere in these tales. Alien characters are usually strangely-featured humanoids with the ability to communicate telepathically with the human characters; they are concessions to plot, and serve to expedite 'the action'. As in all of Smith's science fiction, the scientific element is restricted to no more than the use of certain 'buzzwords' and catch-phrases ("magnetic", "dynamo", "ultra-cosmic rays", etc.), but science and gadgetry generally play more prominent roles in these stories.

"The City of the Singing Flame" (1931, OST) falls squarely into the first category of stories and is one of Smith's most successful works in any genre. It carries a profound and pervasive magic, a high sense of wonder and mystery, and has impressed writers as diverse as Ray Bradbury and Harlan Ellison with its excellence.

The tale consists of the diary of Giles Angarth, a writer of

---

122. Letter to Derleth, 1 December 1930.

fantastic fiction vacationing alone in the Sierras, who stumbles upon two worn pillars that form a doorway to another world. He makes his way across a purple plain to a city "whose massive towers and mountainous ramparts of red stone were such as the Anakim of undiscovered worlds might build". Housed within is the Singing Flame, a fountain of fire whose strange music "seemed to promise all the impossible splendours of which Angarth's imagination has vaguely dreamt". This music draws exotic, alien pilgrims to the city, where they immolate themselves—with great ecstasy—in the Flame. At the end of the story, Angarth joins them.

Although often combined with its lesser sequel, "Beyond the Singing Flame", we refer to the story as it was originally conceived and published,[123] which corresponds to chapters I-III of the combined version. In its sequel, other adventurers travel to the City of the Flame. They immolate themselves as well but find that the Flame is really a doorway to yet another world. They meet Angarth, who explains the nature of both the City and the Flame to them. Thus this second story does much to dispel the atmosphere of magic and mystery created by the first; and for all its inventiveness, it is an inferior work. Smith had also projected a third story in the sequence, "The Rebirth of the Flame" (SS).

Strong autobiographical elements are apparent in the character and terrestrial setting of "The City of the Singing Flame",

---

123. It should be noted that only through happenstance did the two "Flame" stories appear under the single title "The City of the Singing Flame" in Smith's first Arkham House collection, *Out of Space and Time*. Smith had originally intended to include only the first story but had lost the tear-sheets of its original *Wonder Stories* appearance. He did, however, possess tear-sheets of a more recent British publication in *Tales of Wonder*, where the two stories had been linked together by the editor, Walter Gillings. These he passed on to Derleth, after making some revisions of Gillings' interpolating paragraphs.

It may be that Smith understood the dissimilarity of the two "Flame" stories; at any rate, he had no desire to see them inseparably linked in the way they have become today.

and the escape given Angarth represents the fulfillment of a fantasy for Smith who had long wished for some "escape from the human aquarium".[124] And in actuality, Smith himself had walked along Crater Ridge, the takeoff point for the journey to the land of the Flame, in the late 1920s. "The Ridge is a wild, eerie place, differing wholly in its geology and general aspect from the surrounding region, exactly as pictured in the story. It impressed my imagination profoundly, suggesting almost at first sight the contiguity of some unknown, invisible world to which it might afford the mundane approach and entrance".[125] In the story the terrain is described as looking "like the slag and refuse of Cyclopean furnaces, poured out in pre-human years, to cool and harden into shapes of limitless grotesquerie".

Smith's intention with this story was to create an air of verisimilitude for a fundamentally wondrous experience. One of his many complaints about typical scientific adventures was the matter-of-fact way that characters react when faced with the impossible, and he was determined that "The City of the Singing Flame" not share this fault. He worked a 'realism' of character reaction into "The City of the Singing Flame" in order to give Angarth's adventure some power and credibility. Because Angarth experiences a full range of emotions—fear, timidity, alienation, confusion, and disorientation, as well as exaltation and rapture—the level of the reader's involvement in the narrative is deepened.

In the description of Angarth's first journey through the pillars, Smith makes an interesting use of credible character reactions. He begins by invoking a familiar experience: "Nothing is more disconcerting than to miscalculate the degree of descent in taking a step. Imagine, then, what it was like to step forward on level, open ground, and find utter nothingness underfoot!" Confusion, not exhilaration or adventurousness, characterizes Angarth's first moments in the new world, together with feel-

---

124. Letter to Lovecraft (#20, LL), ca. 27 January 1931.

125. "Planets and Dimensions" (PD).

ings of dislocation and the "ghastly sense of separation from all the familiar environmental details that give colour, form and definition to our lives".

Several paragraphs follow that detail Angarth's visual impressions of the landscape. A description of his emotional state then follows: "I felt only a wild desire to escape from the maddeningly oppressive bizarrerie of this region and regain my own world. In an effort to fight down my agitation, I tried to figure out, if possible, what had really happened". Only at this point does Angarth engage in speculation or reasoning, and this is a deliberate move on Smith's part: by not providing an immediate explanation for what has befallen the story's main character, Smith forces the reader to concern himself entirely with Angarth's sensations and emotions. As a result, the reader is drawn more fully into the strange experience. Ray Bradbury had this technique in mind when he wrote that Smith "encloses his characters, and therefore his readers, in a scene, an atmosphere, providing a frame of reference. Once you have trapped your reader in sights, sounds, smells, and texture...no matter how high, wide or grotesque the miracles you introduce, your readers are unable to resist them".[126]

The conclusion of "The City of the Singing Flame" reflects Smith's fascination with loss, or "falls from grace". After his penultimate visit to the land of the Flame, Angarth sees his earthly existence as wan and inadequate beside the glory of a fiery death in the Flame: "literature is nothing more than a shadow. Life, with its drawn-out length of monotonous, reiterative days, is unreal and without meaning, now, in comparison with the splendid death which I might have had". His journal ends, "Tomorrow, I shall return to the city...." Angarth must seek to regain the splendor he has lost.

At one point Angarth admits that "the world about me" (i.e., the mundane world) "seems hardly less improbable and

---

126. Introduction by Ray Bradbury, dated 7 April 1957, to Smith's projected paperback collection, *Far from Time*. In modified form, this piece was used as an introduction to IM.

nightmarish than the one which I have penetrated in a manner so fortuitous"—the unheard-of realm of the Flame is no less real to him than his everyday life. "A Star-Change" (1932, GL) pursues these questions of alternate realities and of illusion versus substance. Like "The City of the Singing Flame", we again are given a solitary man, Lemuel Sarkis, hiking through mountains. He encounters two strange beings on a lonely ridge, aliens so imaginatively conceived that they must rank high in the annals of science fiction's non-anthropomorphic life-forms:

> Each of the beings was about four feet high, with a somewhat doubtful division into head and body. Their formation was incredibly flat and two dimensional; and they seemed to float rather than stand, as if swimming through the air. The upper division, which one accustomed to earthly physical structures would have taken for the head, was much larger than the lower, and more rotund. It resembled the featureless disk of a moonfish, and was fringed with numberless interbranching tendrils or feelers like a floral arabesque.... The lower division suggested a Chinese kite. It was marked with unknown goblin features.... It ended in three broad streamer-like members, subdividing into webby tassels, that trailed on the ground but seemed wholly inadequate for the purpose of legs.

These creatures bring Sarkis to their home world, Mlok, where he is overwhelmed by the unearthly sights, sounds and other sense impressions. Shortly he becomes disoriented, and experiences "an inexpressible malaise, a frightful mixture of confusion, irritation and depression to which all his senses contributed". Smith had long been convinced that "transportation to an alien world would be an experience of utmost terror and strangeness for human nerves, and the probable result would be delirium and madness".[127]

To relieve this anguish, his hosts perform an operation that modifies Sarkis' senses, making them more similar to those of the planet's inhabitants. The world he sees upon awakening bears no resemblance to the intolerable milieu he first beheld, but is exotic and wondrous. He has become the recipient of many new or expanded senses: "He saw new colors of supernal softness and beauty.... One of these [new senses] can best be described as a combination of hearing and touch.... Another sense was that of audible color". (Unfortunately, Smith seemed unable to imagine, or at least describe, new senses that were not simply combinations of the familiar five.)

Sarkis[128] remains on Mlok for a time, but when disaster threatens the planet he is forced to return to Earth, in a haste that prevents the reverse surgical procedure from taking place. Back on Earth, Sarkis' new sensory powers reveal to him an unrecognizable world of horror:

> Around him, in a sullen light, he saw the looming of dark, chaotic masses, whose very contours were touched with nightmare menace. Surely this place was not his studio room—these crazily angled cliffs that closed him in were not walls, but the sides of some infernal pit! The dome above, with its dolorously distorted planes, pouring down a hellish glare, was not the sky-lighted roof that he recalled. The bulging horrors

---

127. Letter to Lovecraft (#5, LL), 9 January 1930.

128. Sidney-Fryer offers an interesting interpretation of this name: "So often Smith's proper names give us excellent clues as to the type of characterization of his heroes. Lemuel Sarkis is no exception—like Lemuel Gulliver (CAS was very fond of the excellent satire, *Gulliver's Travels*), Lemuel Sarkis is also a traveller but on a far greater scale: the 'Sark' in his name has...reference to the Greek root of *sark* or *sarkos*, that is, flesh" (private communication). Sarkis is thus to be seen as a voyager through the realm of the physical, fleshly senses.

that rose before him along the bottom of the pit, with obscene forms and corrupt hues, were surely not his easel, table and chairs.

He is eventually diagnosed as suffering from *delirium tremens* and is committed to an asylum, where to the consternation of the doctors he "persists in dying".

"A Star-Change" expresses several ideas of prime interest to Clark Ashton Smith. Foremost, there is the romantic lure of new senses, to know sensual glories inexperienced and unexperienceable by human beings, to see the universe as a god might see it. And that both Mlok and Earth appear so different to Sarkis after his operation drums home Smith's belief that reality stands upon a shifting, unstable ground defined by our senses. However, Smith is careful to avoid saying that humanity alone is hidebound and sense-blinded, for the Mlokians may be as far from 'the truth' as mankind: "Whether or not his new mode of cognition was closer to ultimate reality, he could not know. It mattered little". Smith also felt that the story stood out for its originality and honesty: "As far as I know, it is almost the only attempt to convey the profound *disturbance* of function and sensation that would inevitably be experienced on an alien world".[129] And on a final note, "A Star-Change" may have influenced Robert Silverberg's novels *Thorns* (1967) and The *Man in the Maze* (1969), in which characters are surgically altered by the inhabitants of the worlds they visit.

"The Light from Beyond" (1931-32, LW), another of Smith's quality science fiction tales, has much in common with "The City of the Singing Flame" and "A Star-Change". All three feature autobiographical characters (a writer of fantastic fiction, two illustrators of fantastic fiction, each of whom encounters something strange in California mountains), the introduction of new senses or new realities, and the presence of wondrous scenes and happenings. All end pessimistically; in each story

---

129. Letter to Derleth, 23 May 1933.

the main character suffers some kind of loss. Like "The City of the Singing Flame" the emphasis of these stories is on unfathomable mysteries and the notion that exotic vistas lie unseen but close at hand.

Although published as "The Light from Beyond" by *Wonder Stories*, Smith's own title for the tale had been "The Secret of the Cairn" (he once complained that the magazine's editors "seem to have a mania for changing titles"[130]). The story begins with strange nocturnal phenomena witnessed by Dorian Weirmoth, a solitary Sierran artist. Wheels of light seem to emanate from behind a nearby ridge; his valley is filled with a strange incense; he hears "a faint music... like the breathing of fairy flutes, ethereally sweet, thrilling, eldritch". He finds a newly-built cairn atop the ridge, which he is unable to approach; and the vegetation around the cairn is strangely mutated. No explanation is provided for these happenings; there is only mystery.

Later a group of "diaphanous... birdlike" beings arrive atop the ridge. They remove something from the cairn, an object "drab, oval, and about the size of a falcon's egg. I might have deemed it no more than a common pebble, aside from one peculiar circumstance: a crack in the larger end, from which issued several short, luminous filaments". Weirmoth inadvertently accompanies the beings to their "infinite world", where the egg or seed grows into a fan of energy like a tree:

> The thing was a fountain of unsealed glories, an upward-rushing geyser of emerald and opal.... The foliage spread like a blown spray of jewels. The plant became colossal, it towered with a pillar-thick stem, and its leafage meshed the five suns.... I saw the fruiting of the tree: the small globules, formed as of blood and light.

---

130. Letter to Derleth, 9 April 1931.

After he eats one of the fruits of the tree, Weirmoth's senses expand and develop in the manner of Sarkis' after his operation, and he undergoes a transition to an omniscience and godhood reminiscent of the Emperor of Dreams in "The Hashish-Eater": "I rose into spheres ulterior and superior. Infinities were rolled before me, I conned them as one cons an unrolled map. I peered down upon the utmost heavens.... I possessed a million eyes and ears.... I recall...the flowering of thoughts into stars and worlds".

But like the tree "that had sprung from the mated energies of earth and the celestial Otherworld", and like the fruits of the tree, formed of an equal mixture of "blood and light", the essence of Weirmoth is divided between the terrestrial and the ultra-terrestrial. The halves split, and Weirmoth becomes two: "I seemed to lose and leave behind me the colossal, shadowy god that still towered above the stars.... I, who beheld the alter ego, was aware of a dark and iron weight, as if some grosser gravity had claimed me". His terrestrial self is returned to earth, and evermore he is "a mere remnant of [his] former self...a clod", haunted by visions of the other world.

In "The Monster of the Prophecy" (1929, OST), the elements of wonder found in the previous stories are tinged with satire. The story was one of Smith's favorites; he called it "the result of a definite inspiration", "absolutely novel in interplanetary fiction", "hilariously satiric in its implications".[131] The hero, Theophilus Alvor, is a country poet trying to make a name for himself in New York City (a fantasy of Smith's?). Unable to market his work, he is on the verge of tossing himself from the Brooklyn Bridge when he encounters Vizaphmal, an alien wizard in human semblance, who takes him to Satabbor, a planet of Antares. After many adventures there, Alvor chooses to remain on the alien planet rather than return to the inhospitable Earth. Smith plotted a sequel, "Vizaphmal in Ophiuchus" (SS), which would have chronicled further adventures of the

---

131. Letters to Lovecraft, 9 January 1930 (#5, LL), and 10 December 1929 (#4, LL); letter to Derleth, 1 December 1930.

Antarrean wizard. The story would have had no human characters.

Central to the plot of "The Monster of the Prophecy" is an idea Smith used in several other satires—the idea of momentous events triggered by misinterpretation, blundering, or pure chance. These events are often mistakenly seen in a religious light and take the form of omens or heavenly visitations; here he is clearly satirizing the solemn mysteries and miracles of terrestrial religions. Alvor is brought to Satabbor to fulfill an ancient prophecy, in which a wizard enters the city of Sarpoulom in the company of "a white monster" possessing two arms and two legs. He accompanies Vizaphmal to the city, the presiding government falls, and Vizaphmal is proclaimed the ruler. Other examples of this sort of satire are found in "The Door to Saturn", in which Eibon and Morghi inadvertently serve as misunderstood prophets for a succession of Saturnian races, and "The Letter from Mohaun Los", in which a temporary fault in Malgraff's time-space sphere causes the device to fall upon a group of soldiers engaged in battle. The crushing of this group is taken as a godly judgment, and the tide of the battle turns.

At several points in "The Monster of the Prophecy" we are treated to passages of exotic description, which Smith used to emphasize the fabulous nature of Alvor's adventure and to sustain an unearthly atmosphere. The details of an Antarrean meal, for instance, would have fit well within the dense, extravagantly imaginative "Hashish Eater":

> The foods were beyond belief in their strangeness, for they included the eggs of a moth-like insect large as a plover, and the apples of a fungoid tree that grew in the craters of dead volcanoes.... Likewise he was given, in shallow bowls, a liquor made from the blood-like juice of living plants, and a wine in which the narcotic pollen of some night-blooming flower had been dissolved.

The story also provides some model examples of Smith's heavy use of metaphor to deepen the emotional significance of a situation. When Vizaphmal first drops his illusion of human form and reveals his true appearance,

> Alvor had the sensation of standing on the rim of prodigious gulfs, on a new earth beneath new heavens; and the vistas of illimitable horizons, fraught with the multitudinous terror and manifold beauty of an imagery no human eye had ever seen, hovered and wavered and flashed upon him....

With its talk of profound gulfs and limitless horizons, the imagery used above is extremely characteristic of Smith.

Some shortcomings of "The Monster of the Prophecy" must also be mentioned. A fine line exists between the satire of hackwork and hackwork itself, and although this line may have been clearly drawn in Smith's mind, the reader is not certain what to take seriously in this tale. Vizaphmal's initial conversations with Alvor are unquestionably the weakest and most unconvincing moments of the story:

> "But who are you?" exclaimed Alvor....
> "I am not a human being", rejoined the stranger, "even though I have found it convenient to don the semblance of one for a while just as you or another of your race might wear a masquerade costume. Permit me to introduce myself: my name, as nearly as can be conveyed in the phonetics of your world, is Vizaphmal, and I have come from a planet of the far-off mighty star that is known to you as Antares".

Alvor's acceptance of Vizaphmal's offer to visit Satabbor is equally rushed and unbelievable. These passages may have been intended as satires of the genre, or may simply represent trite, second-rate writing.

The story also witnesses the introduction of yet another dreadful *deus ex machina*. After the government of Vizaphmal falls, Alvor is seized by the local priesthood who torture him as an abomination against nature. In the midst of his ordeal, however, a meteor strikes the inquisitorial building, killing everyone but himself. Alvor is then free to seek a more even-tempered clime. Perhaps this is a bit of anti-religious irony? Possibly; but other stories certainly demonstrate Smith's willingness to invoke implausible rescues or unlikely coincidences simply to move the plot along.

One final aspect is worth noting, namely that the character of Alvor parodies what Smith saw as his own position in life. Alvor's "old-fashioned classic verses, in spite (or because) of their high imaginative fire, had been unanimously rejected both by magazines and book firms". And soon after arriving on Satabbor, Vizaphmal warns Alvor: "You will be doomed to a certain loneliness among us: you will always be looked upon as a monster, a portentous anomaly; but such, I believe, was your lot in the world where I found you.... There, as you have learned, all poets are regarded as no less anomalous than double-headed snakes or five-legged calves".

"Master of the Asteroid" (1932, TSS) departs from the autobiographical pattern established in the stories discussed so far, and while it bears the trappings of conventional science fiction, the story remains an exceptional mood piece. It is told in diary form, and Smith uses the medium to ably convey an atmosphere of isolation and fear, a sense of ghastly separation from the terrestrial and of the unknown horrors of space. A rocket crashes on a small asteroid. The sole survivor, unable to leave the ship and with supplies dwindling, discovers that life exists in the valley surrounding him. The dominant creatures resemble huge 'walking-stick' insects and seem to worship him as some kind of god (Smith's first title for the story was "The God of the Asteroid"), but here we find no religious satire. No communication with the aliens can be established.

The seasons of this small world last only a few days, and the survivor witnesses a cycle of the life and death of his worshippers. One day an even stranger creature appears, and after its mist-like tentacle passes through the crystal view port, the survivor's diary abruptly ends. The ship, surrounded by the husks of the insect creatures, and containing a staring, desiccated corpse, is found by a later expedition.

It is significant that Smith wrote less frequently for the "stf" magazines as his career as a fictioneer matured. By the time he had begun to withdraw from fiction-writing in 1933-1934, his science fiction had all but disappeared, while he continued to write sporadically of Zothique, Averoigne, and Hyperborea. This was due in part to the falling out he had had with *Wonder Stories*, his most lucrative market for science fiction,[132] but Smith had never really been comfortable writing for any of the science fiction magazines. In an article calling Smith "The Poet of Science Fiction", Arthur Hillman wrote that "he and a few others were fighting a losing battle against the latest trend of heavy science which, with the growing awareness of the social and mechanical aspects of science fiction, brought a decline in tales of ingenuous wonder".[133] For a time Smith fought this decline through his essays and, by example, through his fiction.

Smith, of course, recognized the irony of his position, as a fantasy writer tailoring his products for the science-fiction market. After selling "The Eternal World" to *Wonder Stories*, he shared a chuckle with August Derleth: "Gemsback... advised me to put 'more realism' into my future stories, saying that the late ones were 'verging dangerously on the weird.' That's really quite a josh—as well as a compliment".[134]

---

132. Aside from the publication of the adulterated "Dweller in the Gulf", in May of 1934 Smith engaged the services of a New York attorney to secure $769 in late payments from *Wonder Stones*.

133. Arthur F. Hillman, "The Poet of Science Fiction" (see Sec. Bib.).

134. Letter to Derleth, 21 November 1931.

CHAPTER NINE
PROSE-POEMS

Sometime around 1914, Smith began writing prose-poems: short, concise prose works, often only a paragraph or two in length, written in a highly poetic style and usually expressing a single mood, image, fancy, or emotion, in the form of a miniature narrative or parable.[135] Over the next fifteen years, up to the start of his fiction-writing period, he completed fifty-odd such pieces; nearly all are collected in the posthumous volume *Poems in Prose*, edited by Donald Sidney-Fryer, while the few remaining items can be found in *Strange Shadows*.

In introducing his volume, Sidney-Fryer provides a long and interesting history of the prose-poem, tracing its origins with Aloysius Bertrand, through its use by Poe, Rimbaud, Baudelaire, and finally Smith.[136] Sidney-Fryer characterizes the poem in prose at its best as displaying "a terse and artistic unity in which style, subject-matter, and imagery all work toward the central effect, whether subtly or overtly".[137]

In his prose-poems we find the least-fettered display of

---

135. The distinction between Smith's prose-poems and short stories is sometimes blurred, as is the case for "Sadastor", "The Abominations of Yondo", and "Told in the Desert", each of which can be seen as either a brief story or an extended poem in prose.

136. Donald Sidney-Fryer himself has contributed to the genre in his own *Songs and Sonnets Atlantean* (Sauk City, WI: Arkham House, 1971), published under the name Donald S. Fryer, as he was formerly known.

137. Introduction to *Poems in Prose*, p. xvi.

Smith's artistry in fiction, both in terms of literary techniques and choice of subject matter and materials. Here Smith was free to ignore the encumbrances he found in conventional story writing—plot and characterization—and "to present and develop an idea, image, story, or emotional experience without having to bother with rhyme or strict metre or the arbitrary line length of the traditional forms of verse".[138]

The overall thematic integrity of Smith's work is manifested by prose-poems devoted to loss, the passing of greatness, the question of illusion and reality, ennui, and the yearning for the peace of oblivion. Specific connections to Smith's other writings, especially his short stories, are quickly apparent as well. As mentioned earlier, the story "The Demon of the Flower" is literally an extension of the prose poem "The Flower Devil"; such is the case also for "The Planet of the Dead" and "From the Crypts of Memory". The influence of "The Traveller" and "The Muse of Hyperborea" on "The White Sybil" has been noted, as has the notion that the setting of "A Phantasy" formed a precursor to the world of Zothique. Further, the meeting of lovers in "A Dream of Lethe" is echoed in the Zothique tale, "Necromancy in Naat", while the prose-poem "To the Daemon" foreshadows "The Flower-Women", particularly in its image of a woman cradled within the bowl of a flower.

It is unfortunate that space limitations allow a look at only a few of the poems in prose. And it should be emphasized that these works are all pale in summary or quotation: each should be read in full to appreciate its subtleties of mood and imagery.

The primarily mood-oriented prose-poems range in tone from sorrow to exaltation, and many are unabashedly romantic. "The Broken Lute", for example, tells of a minstrel whose lover has grown cold to him, and who, in sadness, smashes his lute upon a path the woman frequents. There, he hopes, she will see it and breathe once more in her heart a secret sigh for their lost love. "The Litany of the Seven Kisses" relates a lover's ritual

---

138. *Ibid.*

and contains some passages of classic beauty ("I kiss thy cheeks, where lingers a faint flush, like the reflection of a rose upheld to an urn of alabaster"). In "The Mithridate" love is likened both to an anecdote and a poison, "a poison doubly lethal, because it kills so slowly, or does not kill at all". In "The Abomination of Desolation" the only travelers who pass unscathed through the specter-ridden desert of Soom are two lovers, who have found "an abiding Eden in each other's eyes" and who, shielded by their love, are spared the horrors of the outer void.

"From the Crypts of Memory", perhaps Smith's most well-known prose-poem, tells of the somber inhabitants of an age-old world, where the dead far outnumber the living, and the people carry on a dim, lifeless existence. Doom is omnipresent; above the world hangs a dying sun. Further, the inhabitants are oppressed by the great accomplishments of their past, which lie undecayed and unsurpassed. Smith expanded this prose-poem into the short story "The Planet of the Dead" (1930, LW), in which the Earthman Francis Melchior, his gaze transfixed upon a star on the horizon, finds himself coexisting as a poet on a planet of that star. The death of the sun has been proclaimed to be a month away, so Melchior, here called Antarion, steals away to one of the numberless cities of the dead to live his last days alone with his lover Thameera. When the sun expires and the cold that falls becomes "a growing agony, and then a merciful numbness, and then an all-encompassing oblivion", Melchior awakens back on Earth, bearing the double sorrow of his own life and Antarion's, and he wonders which existence of the two is the dream.

In "The Demon, the Angel and Beauty", an unnamed narrator asks alternately a demon and an angel about the nature of Beauty. "Is she the heart of day, or the soul of night?" Both reply that they have little actual knowledge: she is a "transcendent Mystery" to one and a "topic of the most frequent and sublime speculation" to the other. The demon concludes that Beauty does not exist, that she is a "web of shadow and delusion, woven by the crafty hand of God"—while the angel suggests that Beauty is God's secret, the thing upon which God meditates, and the reason for which He has "held Himself immanifest to us for so many aeons".

"The Touchstone" tells of a philosopher who has long searched for this fabled talisman, which reveals the true nature of things. He finds it in a very unattractive and ordinary pebble,[139] and using it, he is *disillusioned*: the true world it reveals is one built of dust and skeletons. In the end he throws the Touchstone aside, "preferring to share with other men the common illusions, the friendly mirages that make our existence possible". Here we see, as elsewhere in Smith, the willingness to accept illusion rather than its dubious or horrible counterpart, reality.

In "Narcissus" Smith finds echoes of vanity and self-absorption in the rust-conquered mirrors of perished sybaritic queens and in the once-shining shields of glorious, long-dead warriors, whose "brave and rutilant camp-fires" are centuried dust. The imagery used is heavy with decay; Smith reminds us that Time obliterates our concerns and conceits.

"The Frozen Waterfall" tells of a man who wishes to refind something from long ago, a "many-stranded waterfall... where once we loitered and loved each other well". Instead he finds it locked in ice and thinks of "deterred desires and aspirations, violent longings checked and frozen in their course. And I found in the waterfall the symbol I had sought; and finding it, I was doubly sad.... For was it not the symbol of my soul?"

Was it the symbol of Smith's soul? The frozen waterfall may perhaps reflect his youthful poetic course and ambition, stilled by the changing tide of taste and fashion.

An effective use of parallel imagery is made in "The Sun and the Sepulcher". The first paragraph presents the scene of sunset upon a tomb, the name of whose occupant is "holden awhile from Oblivion" by the strength of white marble. In the second paragraph, Smith writes that "even thus, even thus, and not otherwise" will the light of the waning sun of the future

---

139. This same pebble makes an appearance in the tale of Zothique, "The Black Abbot of Puthuum".

illume the glacial snows of the dead Earth.

One of the most impressive yet uncharacteristic of the prose-poems is "The Corpse and the Skeleton". In its form it is singular, written as a dialogue between a newly-dead corpse and a long-dead skeleton; the ironic and semi-humorous tone it sustains are exceptional; and its observations and witticisms are remarkable for a piece written when Smith was only twenty-two. In essence, it tells the skeleton's view of life and death: "'Tis a world of creditors, of which the tomb and the worm are the last.... 'Tis a dull business being dead, for all the number of the traffickers". The newcomer asks: "Where, then... are the heavens of light and hells of fire...?" In silent answer, the body of a priest lies nearby, "whose corpulence diminishes momently, for the pampering of worms". Still, the corpse asks the skeleton is if there is no wisdom to be found in death, and is told:

> Perchance 'tis something to know that bodies are made of dust and water, the last of which is evaporable, and the soul as the vapour thereof; for this is all our knowledge, in spite of much that is known and spoken of by hierophant and philosopher. However, unlike the lore and wisdom of these, it may be crammed without discommodation into one skull.

CHAPTER TEN
VERSE

In view of the mass of Smith's poetry and its complexity, little more can be accomplished in this chapter than to provide an outline of his work in verse together with a few examples.

The *Selected Poems* volume contains over five hundred works, and perhaps as many as two-hundred additional poems remain uncollected or unpublished. The range of his productions is equally tremendous: the verse includes a host of nature studies ("The Cherry-Snows" [ca. 1912], "Autumn Orchards" [1923], "The Old Water-Wheel" [1941]), philosophical pieces ("Transcendence", "Chance" [1923], "Town Lights" [1941]), love poems ("Exotique", "Connaissance" [1929]), satires and parodies ("Tin-Can on a Mountain-Top"), and a few blatantly erotic works ("The Temptation" [1924]).[140] Smith was a traditionalist in poetry and took for his models the romanticists George Sterling, Edgar Allan Poe, Charles Baudelaire, and Ambrose Bierce. As such, he aligned himself with a poetic movement whose day had passed, and which had been superseded by the modernist work of T. S. Eliot, e. e. cummings, and Ezra Pound.

In their construction, Smith's poems are mainly conventional in form and meter, though the 1940s saw him dabbling in haiku, producing such excellent works as "Nuns Walking in the Orchard":

---

140. Unless noted, all poems discussed are collected in *Selected Poems*.

Sable-robed, at noon,
They passed beneath red cherries
Ripening with June.[141]

In terms of their content, Smith's poetry abounds in the themes and imagery we have observed in his prose productions. Nowhere, for instance, is Smith's fascination with classic myth and fable clearer than in "The Masque of Forsaken Gods" (ca. 1912), "In Thessaly" (1935), and the love poem "'Do You Forget, Enchantress?'" (1946). And because Smith took up fiction-writing rather late in life, many important themes made their first appearances in his verse. The prominence of loss in the poetry has already been mentioned. His views on the subject of reality and illusion are effectively summed-up in the poem "Maya" (ca. 1925), named for the Hindu goddess or symbol of earthly illusion. "Retrospect and Forecast" (1912) demonstrates an early awareness of the vampiric feeding of life upon death: "Turn round, O Life, and know with eyes aghast / The breast that fed thee—Death, disguiseless, stem: Even now, within my mouth, from tomb and urn, / The dust is sweet". The sense of earlier incarnations of the soul, such as we find in the stories "The Chain of Aforgomon", "Xeethra", and "Ubbo-Sathla", is foreshadowed by poems like "Decadence" (ST,SP):

> By some strange antepast I have consumed
> In a former star foregone the fruits of this;
> And frost and dust commingle in the kiss
> Of love, with my foresaken self entombed.

The many aspects and vagaries of love are the subjects of scores of works, including the poem-cycles "The Jasmine Girdle" and "The Hill of Dionysus" (the former was written in the 1920s for Genevieve Sully; the latter commemorates

---

141. It can be noted that Smith's Boulder Ridge acreage bordered upon a Catholic Novitiate, which he referred to playfully as "the Nunnery of Averoigne".

Smith's friendship in the 1940s with Madelynne Greene and Eric Barker). While many of the love-poems are purely ecstatic ("Psalm",[142] "One Evening"), a host of others ("Sestet", "Selenique" (1923), "Canticle") carry some contrasting element of weariness, sorrow, or bitterness. For example, love in "A Psalm to the Best Beloved" is equated with peace—but it is the peace of oblivion, a shelter from the horrors of the world:

> Thy loosened hair is a veil
> For the weariness of mine eyes and eyelids,
> Which have known the redoubled sun
> In a desert valley with slopes of the dust of white marble
> And have gazed on the mounded salt
> In the marshes of a lake of dead waters.
> Thy body is a secret Eden
> Fed with Lethean springs,
> And the touch of thy flesh is like to savor of lotos.

By contrast, a respite from love itself is wished for in "Amor Aeternalis":

> Away! I know the weariness and fever—
> Kisses compounded of the world's old dust
> With fire that feeds the seventh hell for ever!
> The grave shall keep a gentler couch than thine,
> Though round my heart the roots of nettles twine,
> Wreathed in the ancient attitude of lust.

However, it is Smith's macabre and fantastic poetry that has caught the fancy of most of his readers. Although Smith produced poems of this kind throughout his creative life, a spectral mood is predominant in the collections *Incantations* (published only as a section in *Selected Poems*) and *The Dark Chateau*, in the same sense that cosmic imagery is common to the poems

---

142. Written under the pseudonym, "Chistophe des Laurieres".

of *The Star Treader*. *Incantations* consists of verse composed both before and after Smith's venture in weird-fiction; some of the poems ("The Envoys", "Tolometh", "The Satumienne") tell miniature tales, and could easily have sprung from ideas slated for future short stories. An echo of the fantastic is heard even in the nature studies from this period. In the poem "Lichens" (1929), for instance, Smith writes:

> Old too they seem and with the stones coeval—
> Fraught with the stillness and the mystery
> Of time not known to man;
> Like runes and pentacles of a primeval
> Unhuman wizardry
> That none may use or scan.

Of the many macabre poems Smith produced, a few might be singled out for their excellence. The early work in blank verse, "Medusa" (1912), is a masterpiece of mood and imagery, describing the desolate land wherein the Head of the Gorgon is hidden. The sonnet "The Eldritch Dark" (ca. 1912) tells of the world at nightfall, when, with the setting of the moon and the coming of total dark, "The night grows whole again.... The shadows rest, / Gathered beneath a greater shadow's wings". In the powerful later poem, "Revenant", a specter returns to haunt the dead and empty world that had been his in life, eons ago.

Smith's acknowledged masterpiece in fantastic verse, however, is "The Hashish-Eater, or The Apocalypse of Evil", which he considered "a study in the possibilities of cosmic consciousness".[143] It is believed that this 576-line epic was completed over a period of just ten days, early in 1920. In its use of a succession of invented settings, the poem may have been influenced by Sterling's "A Wine of Wizardry" (1907), which Smith is known to have admired.

The "hashish" of the title is used as a symbol only, repre-

---

143. Letter to S. J. Sackett, 11 July, 1950.

senting one means of obtaining a widening of perspective. In the poem's oft-quoted opening lines, the narrator proclaims the power and glory that a cosmic perspective has given him: "Bow down: I am the emperor of dreams; / I crown me with the million-colored sun / Of secret worlds incredible, and take I / Their trailing skies for vestment when I soar, / Throned on the mounting zenith, and illume the spaceward-flown horizon infinite". In world after world, the narrator witnesses a seemingly inexhaustible set of fabulous scenes and situations.

> Surveyed
> From this my throne, as from a central sun,
> The pageantries of worlds and cycles pass;
> Forgotten splendors, dream by dream, unfold
> Like tapestry, and vanish; violet suns,
> Or suns of changeable iridescence, bring
> Their rays about me like the colored lights
> Imploring priests might lift to glorify
> The face of some averted god....

The visions include an attack by dwarfs upon the Titans; the destruction of a Saturnian palace by a hellish tree which has taken root in the flagstones; a scene which would later provide the basis for the story "The Demon of the Flower"; and the penning of a roc upon the moon, caught so as to pluck "from off his saber-taloned feet / Uranian sapphires fast in frozen blood, / And amethysts from Mars". As the narrator's mastery deepens, he is able to merge with the characters he sees, and to participate in their momentous undertakings.

Suddenly, amidst his wanderings, he hears a note of discord or challenge that he cannot identify but which destroys his fancied omniscience: "all my dreams / Fall like a rack of fuming vapors raised / To semblance by a necromant". The moment of insecurity passes, however, and the journey through the worlds is resumed. But now he finds that his visions have become tainted and hostile and that he cannot control them. In one scene he takes refuge in a magnificent castle but finds within it a monstrous throned Worm, "tumid with all the rottenness of kings".[144] He is pursued thereafter by a horde of monsters (many drawn from classical mythology) summoned "from all the dread spheres that knew my trespassing".

In the end, 'the emperor of dreams' is driven to the edge of an abyss, where all things end. There he is overwhelmed by the strangeness and alienage of his visions and is consumed by the "huge white eyeless Face / That fills the void and fills the universe". Smith explained that this represented "the face of infinity itself, in all its awful blankness",[145] a symbol of the indifference or (perceived) hostility of the realms outside human experience. Like the characters of "The White Sybil" and "The Light from Beyond", the narrator has proven himself incapable of mastering the powers of other spheres, and of containing or understanding the unearthly vistas opened to him.

The judgment made against Mankind, and our ignorance and *hubris*, is a profoundly negative one. At the same time, the tale told by the poem is extravagantly colorful and imaginative. In this way "The Hashish-Eater" serves to encapsulate, as well as any other single work, the artistry and temperament of Clark Ashton Smith.

---

144. This idea/image of a throned Worm reappears almost fifteen years later in his historical fantasy "A Tale of Sir John Maudeville" (as we have seen) and the Hyperborean story "The Coming of the White Worm".

145. From "The Argument of the Hashish-Eater" (SS), Smith's summary of the poem.

PART TWO
SEVEN SUPPLEMENTARY ESSAYS
AND
ONE INCAUTIOUS
COLLABORATION

CHAPTER ELEVEN
THE SONG OF THE NECROMANCER: "LOSS" IN CLARK ASHTON SMITH'S FICTION

The writings of Clark Ashton Smith display a continuity of idea and image that can only be described as remarkable. Fantastic settings and happenings from his early poems crop up twenty years later as the bases for short stories; prose-poems written in Smith's mid-twenties were fleshed into the elaborate fictions of his forties; he would write of Medusa in 1911, in his verse masterpiece "Medusa", and in 1957, four years before his death, in the ironic tale "The Symposium of the Gorgon". Evidence for the interconnectedness of Smith's literary output is discernible in nearly every poem and story. The endurance of this imaginative vision should give us all pause.

Equally impressive is the tenacity with which Smith clung to certain emotional themes throughout his work; and of these themes, he returned most frequently to "loss".

Perhaps a quarter of Smith's fantastic stories (twenty-five or thirty out of some 110) deal in a basic fashion with the subject of loss, and in this essay we shall concern ourselves with the most prominent of these; but nearly every Smith tale and many of his poems make some reference to loss, or use an image of loss metaphorically to set an emotional tone.

In this article attention will be paid to the types of loss we find in Smith's fiction (with some discussion as to why he chose to present those types), and to his attitude towards attempts to regain whatever was lost. The structure of the essay has been inspired by "The Song of the Necromancer", a poem in Smith's jotting notebook, *The Black Book*, that seems to encapsulate nearly all the major aspects of his relationship to loss. The poem strikes me as a piece of some importance for an understanding of Smith's work in fiction:

> I would recall a forfeit woe,
> A buried bliss; my heart is fain
> Ever to seek and find again
> The lips whereon my lips have lain
> In rose-red twilights long ago.
>
> Lost are the lands of my desire,
> Long fled, the hours of my delight,
> The darkling splendor, fallen might:
> In aeons past, the bournless night
> Was rolled upon my rubied pyre.
>
> In far oblivion blows the desert
> Which was the lovely world I knew.
> Quenched are the suns of gold and blue....
> Into the nadir darkness thrust,
> My world has gone as meteors go....

Coming from a man whose tales abound with mages and wizards, and who had a poetic image of himself as a solitary sorcerer (an entire cycle of his personal love-poems was to have been called "Wizard's Love"), the poem's title is a very suggestive one. In fact, "The Song of the Necromancer" is Smith's own "song".

Like any writer who has ever had to scramble to provide motivation for some character, Smith used loss as a plot-element in several of his tales, including "The Ghoul", in which a man's despair over the death of his wife drives him to bargain with a demon; "The Flower-Women", wherein Maal Dweb's yearning for his action-filled youth leads him to challenge the denizens of an untamed world; and "Thirteen Phantasms", whose main character is plagued by bizarre hallucinations of his lost beloved. But for Smith there was an importance to loss that went far beyond plot: his real interest was not in what loss could make his characters *do*, but in how it could make them *feel*.

Smith created scores of situations in which individuals lose the things closest to their hearts, and live on only to regret their loss and to contrast their fallen state with the glory they once knew. He gave his characters the capacity to realize the extent of their loss, and to express the pain they felt; and he used their scrutiny—their comparisons of 'now' and 'then', of 'what once had been' and 'what is no more'—to spotlight the emotions he wished to convey to his readers.

These emotions, attendant to 'falls from grace' of one sort or another, were very special to Smith, and he worked all their shadings and manifestations into his literary output: regret, nostalgia, homesickness, alienation, grief, ennui, loss of innocence, age, death, decay. Certain verbs and adjectives literally ring in our ears after a session with his stories or poems, so often do we encounter them: "sunken", "faded", "fallen", "lost", "irretrievable", "longing", "yearning", "seeking".

Having just argued for such a central role for 'loss' in Smith's fiction, please permit me a brief aside. You have in your hands, dear reader, to the best of my knowledge, the very first essay to discuss the profound fixation Smith had with 'loss'; I have previously never encountered the word linked to CAS in any context whatsoever. How, then, is it possible that this overarching concern of Smith's literary life had gone entirely unnoticed by generations of his critics? Why has this 'Pattern in Smith's Carpet', so to speak, not been recognized long before now? Good questions; but for all that I might speculate on their answers, my most honest reply really boils down to, 'Beats me'.

But having said that... perhaps it's partly been a case of mistaken identity. This has been the case, I believe, for those critics who view Smith as a writer *preoccupied with Death*.

Fritz Leiber, for example, wrote that "Death in all its phases—from maggot-banquets to mere forgetting, erasing forever from all tables of memory—seems to be [Smith's] chief inspiration and theme". This is a misdiagnosis, however—a mistaking of the symptom for the disease. While it may be true (as L. Sprague de Camp would have it) that "no one since Poe has so loved a well-rotted corpse", Death itself was never Smith's fixation. Rather, an individual's death, or the death of a world or a star for that matter, had the potential to open a certain significant door for Smith—a door that could be opened just as easily by 'the passing of years', 'the corruption of innocence', and so on—and through that door would come not Death, but Death's hand-maidens, Yearning and Loss. These were the real subjects of Clark Ashton Smith's obsession, the ground-notes to his emotional life. We hear Smith sounding them clearly, from the mouth of his character 'John Milwarp', writer of imaginative fiction and hero of "The Chain of Aforgomon": "In the background of my mind there has lurked a sentiment of formless, melancholy desire, for some nameless beauty long perished out of time".

Returning to "The Song of the Necromancer", our guidebook to 'loss' in Smith, we cannot help but notice the itemized list of the Necromancer's greatest losses: first up is 'love', followed by 'youth / vigor / power', and lastly 'worlds of impossible splendour'. These three sources of loss will be discussed in turn in this essay. While it is indeed true that the *causes* for his characters' feelings of loss were of lesser interest to Smith than the feelings themselves, this choice of organization is handy, and also provides a ghoulish opportunity for some biographical muckraking. We will take time to look for significant events and circumstances within Smith's own life, the echoes or shadows of which may underlie the loss he crafted into his fiction. We conclude the essay by discussing the fates of those who choose "to seek and find again" whatever they have lost.

* * * * * * *

"...the lips whereon my lips have lain..."

As might be expected of a poet, Smith was greatly attracted to the strength of the emotion of love, and the fervor with which we cling to it and to our lovers. (Note that his love-poems certianly outnumber his more famous "fantastic" or "horrific" poems.) Since it looms so large in our lives, Smith found love an ideal thing for the characters of his stories to lose.

And as it happens, Smith himself had suffered such a loss. Facts are scanty at present, but Smith is known to have fallen in love with "Iris", a "nymph of...harvest-colored hair" (as he said of her in an unpublished poem, "For Iris"), perhaps in the early 1920s. His eventual wife, Carol Jones Dorman, wrote that "he lavished his love upon his first, hopelessly ill beloved, who died of consumption before she was thirty.... And always, after the first tragedy of love for the beautiful blonde separated from her husband ...[Smith] chose brunettes for his deepest loves". (Quotation from an unfinished memoir, *The Man Who Walks the Stars*, in the John Hay Library of Brown University.) And among the poems Smith wrote to or for his Iris, we find the following item, untitled and unpublished, from February 1923:

> Your hair, a memory of gold
> Alone remains from buried years:
> What love was ours, what grief, or happy tears,
> Is now a tale untold.

But Smith would tell the tale of this lost love, veiled and fictionalized perhaps, in many poems and stories.

The textbook example of such a "loss of love" story is "The Venus of Azombeii". The central character of this tale, Julius Marsden, has felt throughout his life "the ineffable nostalgia of the far-off and the unknown" (compare this against Smith's own "wild aspiration toward the unknown, the uncharted, the exotic, the utterly strange and ultra-terrestrial", as he stated it to Lovecraft in October 1930), which compels him to make a journey to dark and mysterious Africa. In a wilderness region he meets a beautiful black woman, Wanaos, whom he comes to love. Marsden experiences a time of wild happiness: "A powerful fever exalted all my senses, a deep indolence bedrugged my brain. I lived, as never before, *and never again,* to the full capacity of my corporeal being.... The world and its fullness were ours" (emphasis added).

As Smith would have it, though, their life together is soon shattered through the treachery of a rival suitor to Wanaos. Both lovers are poisoned with a slow-killing brew, by which, please note, Smith gives them plenty of time to realize the sadness of their fate and the fullness of their loss. "Dead was all our former joy and happiness.... Love, it was true, was still ours, but love that already seemed to have entered the hideous gloom and nothingness of the grave.... The leaden lapse of funereal days, beneath heavens from which for us the very azure had departed ...." Smith shows us the high peak of their love, and in contrast the low ebb of their fallen state.

Identical in its emotions but with a slight twist to its development is the extended prose-poem "Told in the Desert". A young traveller loses his way while crossing a desert expanse. He eventually stumbles upon a cool and fertile oasis where dwells a beautiful girl, Neria. We are told that the young man's sojourn with Neria, like that of Marsden and Wanaos in "Azombeii", was "a life remote from all the fevers of the world, and pure from every soilure; it was infinitely sweet and secure".

Unlike Marsden in "Azombeii", however, the hero of "Desert" abandons his idyllic love-nest, his "irretrievable Aidann", rather than having it taken away from him. But Smith does not end the story there. The man comes to yearn for his "bygone year... of happiness"; and seeking in later years the splendor of the oasis, he is doomed to wander in vain, and all his days thereafter are filled with "only the fading visions of memory, the tortures and despairs and illusions of the quested miles, the waste whereon there falls no lightest shadow of any leaf, and the wells whose taste is fire and madness...."

The next two stories to be discussed, "The Chain of Aforgomon" and "The Last Incantation", have necromancers as their main characters rather than adventurous young men, and possess some other common features to which we will return later.

In "Aforgomon" the sorcerer Calaspa invokes the powers of an evil god to win back a flown hour with his dead beloved, Belthoris. The past is temporarily regained through this necromancy, and in typical fashion Smith presents their resurrected love in the grandest of terms. "We dwelt alone in a universe of light, in a blossomed heaven. Exalted by love in the high harmony of those moments, we seemed to touch eternity". We are left to contrast this with Calaspa's mood after the hour has passed: "Sorrow and desolation choked my heart as ashes fill some urn consecrated to the dead; and all the hues and perfumes of the garden about me were redolent only of the bitterness of death".

"The Last Incantation" contains some of Smith's finest descriptions of the emotions of loss, and the story also serves as a bridge between the "loss of love" and "loss of the past" tales.

At the height of his powers as the mightiest sorcerer of Poseidonis, Malgyris the Mage sees only the empty, unchallenging years ahead of him, and the barren moments of the present, and takes but a cold and hollow joy from his exalted position. Smith's description of this state of mind is worth quoting in full:

> ....and turning from the greyness of the present, from the darkness that seemed to close in upon the future, he groped among the shadows of memory, even as a blind man who has lost the sun and seeks it everywhere in vain. And all the vistas of time that had been so full of gold and splendor, the days of triumph that were colored like a soaring flame, the crimson and purple of the rich imperial years of his prime, all these were chill and dim and strangely faded now, and the

rememberance thereof was no more than the stirring of dead embers.... There was nothing left but shadow and greyness and dust, nothing but the empty dark and the cold, and a clutching weight of insufferable weariness, of immedicable anguish.

Amid this desolation, Malgyris is sustained only by a gentle memory from his innocent youth which "like an alien star ...still burned with unfailing luster—the memory of the girl Nylissa whom he had loved in days ere the lust of unpermitted knowledge and necromantic dominion had ever entered his soul".

Like the male protagonists of the other stories discussed, Malgyris aches for his lost love. Unlike the others, however, his mind also dwells upon the passing of his former, untarnished self, the "fervent and guileless heart" of his youth, and the glorious, sun-filled days of his past. This sentiment leads us to a group of stories featuring Smith's second method for bringing loss and regret into the lives of his characters.

* * * * * * *

"...the darkling splendor, fallen might..."

Smith set his most famous cycle of stories, the tales of Zothique, in a "fallen" world where the past infinitely outweighs the future. "On Zothique, the last continent, the sun no longer shone with the whiteness of its prime, but was dim and tarnished as if with a vapor of blood". There are constant reminders of age and decay, of a glory withered away by Time: vast deserts of tombs and buried cities, frequent references to the greater potency of the potions and spells of elder wizards, etc.

On the level of the individual, Smith dishes out the same bitter brew. His fiction is filled with characters haunted by memories of a more desirable past, from whom Time has stolen precious years. Depending on the character in question—again, Smith's focus is on loss itself, not the object lost—they may desire the power and glory they once knew, the simplicity and vigor of the years of youth, a lost innocence, some splendrous state of being, or the vanished beauty and grandeur of incomparable cultures and beloved worlds. (Here, of course, one notes the title of Smith's second collection of short stories, *Lost Worlds*, originally *The Book of Lost Worlds*.)

Just why Smith was so obsessed with the notion of 'a fall from a past of grace' is a matter for speculation, and we should bear in mind that 'armchair psychoanalyst' is a dubious profession. Still, it is possible that at the time he wrote the bulk of his stories, Smith felt that he had suffered a profound 'fall from grace'. Smith's late teens and early twenties had certainly been a heady period: he'd been taken under the wing of a personal idol, the poet George Sterling, and his first book of poetry had brought him comparisons to Keats and Shelley. This notoriety must surely have raised his standing in his small hometown, not to mention his own expectations for the future. And yet the Depression found Smith without a job or viable occupation, unable to eke out a living as a poet, with girfriends berating him for his lack of ambition. And while his switch to writing fiction for the pulps *did* put bread on the table, he found it a very distatsteful business at times—he once said to Sterling that writing prose was "a hateful task, for a poet, and [one which] wouldn't be necessary in any true civilization". In short, it may be that Smith suffered that variety of 'let-down' or loss peculiar to child prodigies.

As a simple example of this yearning for the past, consider the following paragraph from "The Testament of Athammaus", a story which details the desertion of the Hyperborean capital Commoriom as seen through the eyes of the one-time public executioner.

> Forgive an aged man if he seem to dwell, as is the habit of the old, among the youthful recollections that have gathered to themselves the kingly purple of

removed horizons and the strange glory that illumes irretrievable things. Lo! I am made young again when I
recall Commoriom, when in this grey city of the sunk-
en years I behold in retrospect her walls that looked
mountainously down upon the jungle....

Note that the years after Commoriom are "sunken", and its glory is "irretrievable". Also note that Athammaus is alone in his suffering: "And though others forget, or haply deem her no more than a vain and dubitable tale, I shall never cease to lament Commoriom". While others are healed, Smith chose to center his tale on a man whose feelings of regret have remained strong and vivid.

In "Xeethra", perhaps his most famous tale of Zothique, Smith presents multifold loss alongside monstrous irony. A young goatherd, Xeethra, eats an enchanted fruit and is henceforth tormented by the memories of a past life wherein he was Prince Amero, ruler of the fair kingdom of Calyz. The bewildered and newly awakened king is repelled by the rude and simple life of Xeethra; he longs for a dimly recalled life of opulence. He journeys in search of Calyz, but discovers that the land has become a parched desert. Xeethra/Amero is "whelmed by utter loss and despair" at the sight of his ruined and crumbled homeland.

At this point in the story an emissary from Thasaidon, the Satan of the future, appears and offers him a strange deal. At the price of his soul, the life Amero once knew will be returned to him—but it will remain *only so long as he wishes it to*. Not really understanding this clause, the young man accepts the bond; and suddenly the past lives again for him, and he is the king of a bountiful land. But in time he succumbs to ennui, and finds himself wishing for the simple life of a goatherd. In an instant he is back once more in the leper-peopled desert of Calyz. "His heart was a black chill of desolation, and he seemed to himself as one who had known... the loss of high splendor; and who stood now amid the extremity of age and decay.... Anguish choked the heart of Xeethra as if with the ashes of burnt-out pyres and the shards of heaped ruin.... In the end, there was only dust and dearth; and he, the doubly accursed, must remember and repent for evermore all that he had forfeited", both the powerful life of a monarch, and the carefree and uncluttered life of a shepherd. He can never return to either life.

An even grander scale of suffering arising from 'the loss of the past' is displayed in the prose-poem "Sadastor". On a distant planet, "dim and grey beneath a waning sun...a token of doom to fairer and younger worlds", the demon Chamadis discovers the mermaid Lyspial wallowing in a small briny pool that had once been a far-flung ocean. She has witnessed the slow desiccation of the sea and the destruction of the glorious world of her past; she is tortured with the knowledge of her present state, and of all she has lost.

> "Of the seas wherein I swam and sported at leisure... there remains only this fallen pool. Alas! my lovely seas, with their mingled perfumes of brine and weed.... Alas! the quinquiremes of cycle-ended wars, and the heavy-laden argosies with sails of cordage and byssus.... Alas! the dead captains, the beautiful dead sailors that were borne by the ebbing tide to my couches of amber seaweed.... Alas! the kisses that I laid on their cold and hueless lips...."

Another fallen world is presented in the prose-poem, "From the Crypts of Memory". The setting is a shadowy planet orbiting "a star whose course [was] decadent from the high, irremeable heavens of the past". The people of this world are unspeakably ancient and have fallen far from their golden past. Only in memories can they haltingly recapture "an epoch whose marvelous worlds have crumbled, and whose mighty suns are less than shadow". But such memories only add to the burden of age and sorrow, and by contrast their lives are made to seem even more pale and ghostly: "Vaguely we lived, and loved as in dreams—the dim and mystic dreams that hover upon the verge of fathomless sleep. We felt for our women ...the same desire that the dead may feel".

And it doesn't stop there—for Smith's characters, not even death is an end to yearning and despair. On the contrary: while "a living death" was used in "From the Crypts of Memory" as a metaphor for a great suffering, a literal 'life in death' is employed in "The Empire of the Necromancers" as a tool for generating feelings of loss. The legions of the dead, drawn forth from their tombs to serve as slaves to a pair of necromancers, find themselves living a sort of half-life: "the state to which they were summoned was empty and troublous and shadow-like. They knew no passion or desire, or delight...." We hear of their longings through the resurrected Prince of the people, who "knew that he had come back to a faded sun, to a hollow and spectral world. Like something lost and irretrievable, beyond prodigious gulfs, he recalled the pomp of his reign ...and the golden pride and exultation that had been his in youth.... Darkly he began to grieve for his fallen state". Smith tormented the poor souls of this story with the loss of their glorious pasts, their very lives, and even the peace of oblivion.

* * * * * * *

"...Quenched are the suns of gold and blue..."

Now how do I top that?, Smith must have asked himself. We find his answer in a handful of stories in which individuals lose not simply the past, nor even life itself, but a glory beyond life, some 'unnatural' state or condition. In every case the 'unnatural state of being' is an ecstatic and desired one, and of course this makes perfect sense: Smith wanted his characters to *long* for the splendor they had experienced, beside which everyday life is wan and inadequate. And given such glorious experiences, they would naturally make the contrasts and comparisons of 'then' and 'now' that Smith liked to use, and feel the kind of regret and empty despair that so fascinated him.

The visions presented to these hapless characters are often so completely strange and wondrous that they can only be seen or understood in part. They are too far beyond the mundane sphere of human experience, like the image of incarnate Beauty glimpsed in Smith's poem "A Dream of Beauty": "Her face the light of fallen planets wore, / But as I gazed, in doubt and monderment, / Mine eyes were dazzled, and I saw no more". This itself is a technique Smith used to intensify and magnify the contrast of the inconceivable state of being, and the return to commonplace reality.

Stories in this category include "The City of the Singing Flame", "The End of the Story", "The Light from Beyond", and "The White Sybil". There is no need to describe the distinct wonders found in each of these tales. We need only note the similarity of their characters' attitudes as they 'come off the high' of their unique experiences:

> Words are futile to express what I have beheld and experienced.... Literature is nothing more than a shadow. Life, with its drawn-out length of monotonous, reiterative days, is unreal and without meaning, now.... ("The City of the Singing Flame")

> I have forgotten much of the delirium that ensued.... There were things too vast for memory to retain. And much that I remember could only be told in the language of Olympus.... Infinities were rolled before me.... I peered down upon the utmost heavens.... I am a mere remnant of my former self.... ("The Light From Beyond")

> Of all that followed, much was forgotten afterwards by Tortha. It was like a light too radiant to be endured.... ever afterward there was a cloudy dimness in his mind, a blur of unresolving shadow, like the dazzlement in

eyes that have looked on some insupportable light. ("The White Sybil")

For the heroes of these stories this past glory shall always be more resplendent and desirable than either the present or the future, a time always to be longed for. And for some it is a thing they must try to regain, whatever the cost.

****

"...I would recall...a buried bliss..."

"The Song of the Necromancer" has been our general guidebook to Smith's relationship to loss, and we take note that it begins with a declaration of intent: the unhappy sorcerer (we learn of his unhappiness in the subsequent stanzas) would seek to resummon his lost past, and to draw back his dead love from the tomb. As we have seen, the same is true of several of the characters we find in Smith's short stories.

Why Smith should have them strive to recapture what they've lost is obvious—such striving serves to underscore their unhappiness, and the depths of their dissatisfaction. That all these attempts either fail or end in self-destruction reflects Smith's generally pessimistic outlook. "You can never go home again", he's telling us, "it's no longer there". Or if it is still there, and somehow you succeed in making it back, the achievement will amount to a very mixed blessing.

In a story like "Told in the Desert" what is sought after is literally unattainable, for though he may search the desert for the rest of his life, that young man will never again find the fertile oasis in which he lived so happily with Neria.

What Malgyris seeks in "The Last Incantation" is just as unattainable, though more figuratively so. Believing that he would be content to have his lost Nylissa beside him again, he summons her spectre from the grave. Once she has materialized, however, he begins to find fault with her manner and appearance. Dissatisfied and unsettled, he dismisses the phantom, at which point his familiar explains the true nature of his yearning and its predestined failure: "No necromantic spell could recall for you your own lost youth or the fervent and guileless heart that loved Nylissa, or the ardent eyes that beheld her then".

This same lesson is learned in Smith's unfinished tale "Mnemoka". Space-Alley Jon, a drifter of the space-lanes, purchases an illicit Martian drug which brings back memories with all the strength of real experiences. Jon intends to relive his first sexual experience, back in his innocent adolescence, with a girl named Sophia: "The thrill of that yielding... removed in time by years spent on half the solar worlds... remained poignant in memory". But after downing the drug, he is haunted instead by visions of a brutal murder he recently committed. His life has become too soiled to allow retrieval of the moment he longed for. The boy who had lain with Sophia no longer existed. Jon, like Malygris, has learned that the same river can never be crossed twice.

Calaspa's quest in "The Chain of Aforgomon" is also unsatisfying, and is self-destructive as well. His conjured hour with Belthoris vanishes back into the past just as a temporary spat develops between the two lovers. Ending on such a sour note, he proclaims that "vain, like all other hours, was the resummoned hour; doubly irredeemable was my loss". Equally tragic is the price Calaspa pays, as he knew he must, for casting the time-distorting spell: he is tortured and killed by the local priesthood, and his soul is cursed to travel from body to body into the future, until in some other incarnation he shall die again for his crime.

Indeed, even when the acknowledged price is their own destruction, Smith's men go forward unhaltingly to retrieve what they have lost, so great is their despair. The narrator of "The City of the Singing Flame" ends the tale by saying that he will return to the City and immolate himself in the Flame, that he might merge with the unearthly beauty and music that he had sampled and lost; and the hero of "The End of the Story" makes the same resolution, to die on the couch of a deadly lamia, from which he had been taken by force, rather than live out his years without her love:

> I lamented the beautiful dream of which [I had been] deprived.... Never before had I experienced a passion of such intensity, such all-consuming ardor, as the one I conceived for [the lamia Nycea] ...and I know that whatever she was, woman or demon or serpent, there was no one in all the world who could ever rouse in me the same love and the same delight.

But whether they seek to regain their loss, or choose to suffer through a life of torment and regret, the characters in the stories we've discussed are all made to feel "the loss of high splendor", to live through "sunken years", and to long for the return of "a buried bliss"; and as each is the puppet-creation of Clark Ashton Smith, their songs of woe should be heard as those of the Necromancer himself.

CHAPTER TWELVE
CAS & DIVERS HANDS: IDEAS OF LOVECRAFT AND OTHERS IN SMITH'S FICTION

Considering that Clark Ashton Smith corresponded for years with several of the finest minds in weird fiction, it shouldn't surprise us to learn that some of the ideas and images we encounter in his stories are not his own. Smith regularly mailed manuscripts to his friends H. P. Lovecraft, August Derleth, and Donald Wandrei, and took much of their criticism to heart; but suggestions came also from his editors, and from the Auburn acquaintances to whom he would show his early drafts.

By far the greatest influence was exercised by Lovecraft, reflecting both that writer's intense interest in the theory and structure of fantastic stories, as well as his own great imaginative powers. A handful of examples of Lovecraft's hand in Smith's stories are documented in Lovecraft's *Selected Letters* volumes, and references in Smith's letters to HPL hint at a few more. We will first list these examples, then examine influences from other sources.

In a letter to HPL dated November 23, 1930, Smith outlined a plot germ that was to grow into "The Return of the Sorcerer," involving a murderer who dismembered his victim and is being haunted by the severed parts of the corpse. Lovecraft thought to provide an explanation for the haunting, and simultaneously to expand the story's scope, by introducing a sorcerous background for the two men. This suggestion was adopted by Smith and led eventually to the introduction of the *Necronomicon* into the tale. Around the same time, HPL supplied Smith with the idea of finding an ancient manuscript in English and in one' s own hand, before he himself had incorporated it into "The Shadow out of Time" (see Selected Letter #440). Smith included this idea in his unfinished novelette, "The Master of Destruction," and may in fact have been deterred from completing the yarn, in part, because Lovecraft had gotten around to using the notion so masterfully himself! And it may be, as Derleth points out in his footnote to Selected Letter #673 (November 29, 1933), that a dream of Lovecraft's inspired "The Treader of the Dust," completed February 15, 1935.

An in-joke in Smith's "The Necromantic Tale" revolves around another suggestion from HPL. The main character in the story, a certain Sir Roderick, is spiritually linked to an ancestor who was burned at the stake. He reads a record of the crimes and punishment of this ancestor, his consciousness is propelled backward, he experiences the burning death, and awakens from the "dream" to find that his ankles are scorched. Lovecraft mentioned to Smith that he might have people in the crowd swear they'd seen the figure at the stake disappear, and that this "rumor" might make it into the old record that the contemporary Sir Roderick reads. Smith loved this suggestion, thinking that it "made" the story. So, if you crack open your copy of Smith's *Other Dimensions*, you'll find that in the story this "rumor" was indeed amended to the old document—but we're told the amendment had been written in "a finer hand than the rest" (this could refer to Lovecraft's notoriously small handwriting, or Smith may have been simply complimenting the elder writer).

The extant HPL-CAS correspondence also records that Smith chose not to accept Lovecraft's proposed ending for "A Star Change." In this tale a man is whisked to a far, alien world, where he suffers unspeakable torment at the strange sights and sensations. His hosts perform an operation which transfigures his senses, permitting him to tolerate his surroundings. He eventually escapes back to earth, where these new sense-abilities cause him to perceive everything around him with horror. On the margin of the letter (ca. early October 1930) in which Smith outlined the plight of the main character, HPL jotted down, "Have him find what he thinks to be an utterly strange and hideous planet—recognizing it as the earth (except for vaguely disquieting suggestions of familiarity) only at the last," and passed this on to Smith in Selected Letter #439. However, in the story as Smith wrote it, the hero understands from the first that he has reached the earth.

Beyond Lovecraft, a few other instances are known in which Smith took the advice of others for his fiction. The horrific spice added to the end of "The Resurrection of the Rattlesnake"—finding bloody rattles in the author's fist—carne from a girlfriend. Harry Bates, editor of *Strange Tales*, suggested the repetition of the premature burial in "The Second Interment." The central idea for Smith's unfinished "The House of Haon-Dor" carne from a correspondent, who told him of a haunted shack in Oceanside. For "The Dimension of Chance", Smith admits that "the basic idea—the random atoms, etc.—was suggested by the [*Wonder Stories*] editor" (CAS to Derleth, November 15, 1932). And unknown modifications to the ending of "The Maker of Gargoyles" came from Derleth.

On the opposite end of the stick, CAS offered criticism and plot-twists to his group of pen-pals for stories like "The Return of Hastur", "The Shadow over Innsmouth", and "The Lives of Alfred Kramer", but it seems that his offerings usually fell on deaf ears. In all likelihood, Derleth was too haughty to consider making any changes to his work, and Lovecraft was probably too depressed...

In an article of this sort it seems natural to mention for completeness Smith's acknowledged collaborations, of which there are three. "The Third Episode of Vathek", with William Beckford, represents a story completed by Smith, with no actual collaboration. Smith added 4,000 words to the tale, writing without a synopsis, although he felt "the development Beckford had intended is obvious enough" (CAS to Derleth September 11, 1932). For "Seedling of Mars / The Planet Entity," as by Smith and E. M. Johnston, he worked with a plot by Johnston entitled "The Martian," which had won second place in the *Wonder Stories Quarterly* interstellar plot contest (I wonder who and what won first?)—the *Quarterly* commissioned Smith to write a story around it. And for "The Nemesis of the Unfinished," evidence indicates that Smith first fleshed out one version of this story from a sketch by his friend Don Carter, and later went on to write a variant version of his own devising, keeping only the character of the frustrated writer.

CHAPTER THIRTEEN
THE BIRTH OF UBBO-SATHLA: SMITH, WANDREI, ALFRED KRAMER, AND THE BEGOTTEN SOURCE

Two of the most imaginative and important writers of the 1930s pulp scene were Clark Ashton Smith and Donald Wandrei. Each contributed unique and instantly recognizable fantasies to the magazines of the day, and each had his own small but devoted following. Smith concentrated on transfiguring prose into poetry; Wandrei worked to perfect the language of fear and wonder. Smith took inspiration from the realm of ancient mythology and from flights of pure fancy; Wandrei transplanted the scenes and images of his nightmares into fiction.

To readers familiar with the work of these two men it may seem that "creativity" is the only link between them, the only similarity, but evidence has begun to indicate other connections. We shouldn't be too surprised by this: Smith and Wandrei were friends and correspondents for thirty-five years and read each other's work with great interest. They exchanged many fantastic stories with one another, often in their early, formative states.

Case in point: there is clear evidence, I believe, of a Smith-Wandrei connection for Smith's famous story, "Ubbo-Sathla". Written in February 1932, the tale appeared in the July 1933 Issue of *Weird Tales*, having been accepted by editor Farnsworth Wright in May 1932 on a second submission. It belongs tangentially to Smith's cycle of Hyperborean stories, and involves an ancient crystal sphere, said in *The Book of Eibon* to have the power over time. The title creature, Ubbo-Sathla, is a vast and formless mass, which presided over the fens of the steaming, new-made Earth at the very Beginning of Time. Both Ubbo-Sathla and *The Book of Eibon* were subsequently subsumed into the Cthulhu Mythos.

A certain amount of confusion has arisen as a result of this, particularly in regards to Ubbo-Sathla's epithet (see Robert M. Price's "Beget Me Not" in Crypt of Cthulhu #7, p. 30). August Derleth called him "the unforgotten source" in *The Lurker at the Threshold*, and this is no misprint—Derleth's original typescript for the novel reads "unforgotten". Elsewhere Ubbo-Sathla is referred to as "the unforgotten beginning" or "the unbegotten beginning". But Smith gets the last word, of course: in a quotation from *The Book of Eibon* in "Ubbo-Sathla", we find the creature is "the unbegotten source", i.e., that which was never spawned.

But truth to tell, Ubbo-Sathla was not quite the motherless waif that Smith would have us believe, and this brings us to Donald Wandrei's short story, "The Lives of Alfred Kramer".

Smith read "Alfred Kramer" in manuscript in August 1931, thirteen months before its publication in *Weird Tales*. As is well known, Smith, Lovecraft, Wandrei, and Derleth often used their correspondence to circulate new short stories for criticism. "Alfred Kramer" made it first to HPL, then to Smith; Derleth may have seen it later. Smith seemed genuinely to like the yarn, although he made some suggestions towards revision. But before discussing these, a short description of "The Lives of Alfred Kramer" would be helpful. The story begins with the chance meeting in a smoking car of two late-night train passengers, Alfred Kramer and Wallace Forbes. The narrator, Forbes, is disturbed and oddly repelled by the pale and unmoving face of his new acquaintance, who tells him (rather abruptly) that he fears to fall asleep. Kramer eventually reveals that he is the inventor of the "Kappa Ray", a form of cosmic energy that has the effect upon humans of invoking genetically stored memories of previous lives. He has generated this energy and stored it in a sort of battery, and by exposing himself to it before sleep has induced dreams which are "memories of the past". In his first experimentation with the Kappa Ray, Kramer relived some experiences of his immediate ancestors (his father's flight from the Chicago Fire and his grandfather's shipwreck); subsequent attempts brought him memories of a medieval witch-burning, a Druidic sacrifice, an encounter with Christ, the sinking of Atlantis, and so on.

Unfortunately, at that point in his investigations Kramer discovered that his bodily form had also mimicked the temporal regression: his appearance had become that of a shaggy Neanderthal!

Needless to say, Kramer had resolved to put an end to his sleeping journeys, and in a fit of brutish rage he destroyed the Kappa battery. But he found to his horror that he continued to dream, and that each night drew him farther back along the evolutionary path. He dreamt of the years before the advent of Man, and inhabited the bodies of ever-cruder beasts. In the latest dream he was an invertebrate swimming sluggishly through the tepid and silty seas of Earth's beginning.

Kramer tells Forbes that he has held himself awake for three full days, fearing that the next mental voyage will be his last. A lull in the conversation ensues, however, and Kramer dozes off. Forbes, with some intimation of what is to come, is in the process of 'exiting stage-left' when Kramer screams, jumps up, drops his mask and artificial hands, and dissolves into a pool of that substance near-and-dear to the *Weird Tales* crowd, fetid slime. The end.

Now, the idea of a drug or spell that would propel consciousness backward along the trail of memory was also popular in *Weird Tales*. Frank Belknap Long had used it in "The Hounds of Tindalos", Clark Ashton Smith would build "The Chain of Aforgommon" around the same notion, and Wandrei himself would employ it again in his 1934 story "The Man Who Never Lived". No doubt there are many other examples. But when

Smith read and commented upon Wandrei's story, he had no quarrel with its originality. And although Wandrei didn't actually take Smith's suggestions, it's important for us to know what they were, and to keep them in mind for the following discussions. Writing first to August Derleth, he'd said:

> I criticized "Alfred Kramer" pretty heavily myself, advising Wandrei to simplify the yarn and work in some sort of connecting thread among the ancestral incidents; perhaps a pursuing menace, which Kramer is finally forced to confront in its primordial lair as he goes back on the trail of memory. There seems to be a lack of point and significance as the tale stands; though the underlying notion is certainly a fine one. (Letter dated August 28, 1931)[146]

A letter to Lovecraft expressed the same misgivings, but was perhaps a bit more positive:

> The story is excellent, with a strong ending; but I agree with you that it could be simplified to advantage. I also think that it could be made much more tremendous if there were more unity in the incidents remembered from ancestral lives by Kramer. There might be some recurrent haunting horror in many if not all of them—a horror which Kramer is forced to confront in its primordial lair by going back to the first genesis of organic life on the ' planet—or beyond organic life. (Undated letter.)[147]

(In fact, Smith was proposing a story rather like C. L. Moore's "Tryst in Time", published in the December 1936 issue

---

146. Smith's letter to Derleth: Courtesy of the State Historical Society of Wisconsin.

147. Smith's letter to HPL, and all quotations from synopses: Courtesy of the John Hay Library of Brown University.

of *Astounding*, in which a temporal explorer has a series of adventures in the past, and is met in each by a girl or woman in whom he sees a tantalizing hint of familiarity. It turns out that the man and woman are somehow fated for one another.)

So then, now that we know that Smith read "Alfred Kramer", and held various opinions on it, what does this story have to do with "Ubbo-Sathla"? The evidence for a connection lies in a group of Smith's plot-germs only recently discovered.

Roughly twenty pages of hand-written story synopses came to light in 1981, and were delivered by Smith's literary executors to the Clark Ashton Smith Collection of Brown University in August of that year. The papers date from the period 1930-32 and contain the outlines of many of Smith's most famous tales, as well as scores of ideas that he never finished into stories. One page in particular is relevant to this discussion. This page is also somewhat unique, in that we know without question which is the earlier-written side of the sheet, and which is the later: both the first entry on side one and the last entry on side two outline "The Beast of Averoigne," and while the second occurrence is a complete description of the tale, the first is just a single sentence, representing Smith's initial inspiration. This page contains the following items (dates of story completion, if applicable, are given in parentheses):

Side One:
The Beast of Averoigne (June 18, 1932)
The Inverse Avatar
The Double Shadow (March 14, 1932)
The Cosmic Sequel (may have served as an inspiration for "Double Cosmos", begun in 1934. completed March 1940)
The Embassy to Tiirath

Side Two:
Ubbo-Sathla (February 15, 1932)
The Beast of Averoigne (June 18, 1932)

It seems reasonable to assign this page to the period "late 1931-early 1932," a time shortly following Smith's August 1931 critique of "The Lives of Alfred Kramer".

One of the synopses, "The Inverse Avatar," seems unquestionably to be Smith's rephrasing of "Alfred Kramer", with Wandrei's weak point—as Smith saw it—explicitly corrected:

> A man who remembers his incarnations in the future, and becomes convinced that his own chain of lives is moving backward in time—fleeing from a Nemesis that originated at the world's end, and seeking a primal sanctuary.

In this synopsis we find the notions of (1) a string of incarnations extending from the main character to other times; (2) awareness of these lives via "ancestral memory", however activated; and (3) a flight through these lives from a pursuing menace.

What Smith chose to do with Wandrei's story, and his early suggestions for it, was to play the flip-side, so to speak: rather than having the hero *confront* the pursuing horror in its prehistoric lair, as he'd first suggested, the hero would *seek refuge* in prehistory, far from the post-historic lair of the Thing. He'd added his own twist to the plot-line Wandrei developed in "Alfred Kramer."

Could this "flip side", with its inverted logic, make it as a story? Well, Smith never went on to write it....

...But he did write "Ubbo-Sathla". As that page of synopses indicates, soon after plotting "The Inverse Avatar" he plotted "Ubbo-Sathla", which returns more to the story-line he had envisioned for "Alfred Kramer", but which still contains elements of "The Inverse Avatar":

"Ubbo-Sathla"

> A man who, in trance, goes back in earthly time to the very beginning, when Ubbo-Sathla, the primal one, out of whom all terrestrial life has sprung, lay wallowing in the mist and slime, playing idiotically with the tablets on which are writ the wisdom of vanished premundane gods. In his trance, the man believes that he has been sent to retrieve these tablets; but, approaching Ubbo-Sathla, he seems to revert to some primordial life-form; and forgetting his mission, wallows and ravens with the spawn of Ubbo-Sathla. He does not reemerge from his trance.

In this synopsis as well we find Smith discussing a mental flight backward in time, towards a goal. There is a Nemesis in its primordial lair, which the hero "confronts", and this confrontation does indeed take place at "the first genesis of organic life...or beyond organic life," as his letter to Lovecraft had suggested for "Alfred Kramer". And just like the Wandrei story, the hero of "Ubbo-Sathla" is forced to inhabit the body of a primitive creature.

As I'm sure we all remember from the completed story, the main character Paul Tregardis is an incarnation of the Hyperborean wizard Zon Mezzamalech. (So we see that the concern with "previous' lives" is maintained in "Ubbo-Sathla", as is the notion of the Horror or Nemesis forming the link between them.) A misty globe of crystal, found in a pawn shop, magically connects the two men, whose lives are separated by millions of years. Mezzamalech seeks to retrieve the tablets of elder wisdom that lay beside Ubbo-Sathla, and it is his greed and determination that drags the passive Tregardis into the past, to his destruction.

This emphasis on a character living in the past (Mezzamalech), with a corresponding deemphasis of his future incarnation (Tregardis), represents a holdover from "The Inverse Avatar". In that story's inverted time-sequence, the main character would have been "the man of the past," who knows of his future incarnations.

(As a last aside, we should note that the "memories of future incarnations" concept stayed with Smith a while longer. Six weeks after writing "Ubbo-Sathla" he completed "The Plutonian Drug", in which a man takes a drug that enables him to visualize his future movements as an unbroken chain of self-images—his future selves—extending out of sight.)

None of the above analysis, of course, points to any mimicry or lack of imagination or originality on Smith's part, regarding the genesis and development of "Ubbo-Sathla". Rather, this discussion underscores his creativity—whatever its inspirations, "Ubbo-Sathla" remains very much a story by Clark Ashton Smith.

CHAPTER FOURTEEN
A REVIEW OF *THE DEVIL'S NOOTBOOK*

The Devil's Notebook: Collected Epigrams and Pensees, by Clark Ashton Smith (ed. Don Herron and Donald Sidney-Fryer; Mercer Island, WA: Starmont House, 1991.)

As an inexperienced reviewer of books, I nearly failed to realize the perspective from which this review should be written. I had been thinking that little needed to be said, really, about this collection of Smith's epigrams: such revealing material by Clark Ashton Smith is self-evidently of interest, and its publication can only be welcomed with open arms and uncapped pens. This is still true. But what is also true is that this book will probably hold little value for the majority of Smith's readers, those drawn to Smith as a storyteller or poet, and those who admire the richness of his imagination. For all that Zothique is mentioned at one point amongst these one-liners, this is not a book in which Smith wears his "fantaisiste" hat (or beret). *The Devil's Notebook*, then, fills a niche most closely analogous to that filled by Lovecraft's essays, on politics or domestic animals or dropped eggs or whatever: mere irrelevant verbiage to the Yog-Sothothians, but the very Library of Babel to students of the man. In this case, however, given the relative thinness of *The Devil's Notebook*, we're probably talking "Babelian Reading Room" here.

The epigrams in *The Devil's Notebook* were composed in

the early 1920s, prior to Smith's fiction-writing period but after several poetry volumes had appeared, and were published for the most part in Smith's column for *The Auburn Journal*, his local newspaper. Given the opportunity to have his drops of wisdom—and acid—put into print, Smith skirted the down-home homilies the editors might have expected, and cranked out instead a slew of acerbic jabs. A lot of these little things are tremendously humorous, and many are unquestionably insightful. Equally many are drawn from a side of Smith that is often missing from his other writings, apart from satires like "The Monster of the Prophecy": at a level of intensity which almost shocks us, these epigrams are bitter, anti-social, self-serving, elitist, and sexist (or perhaps "cruel to women" is a better phrase to use than our modem one). The only other source I'm aware of which comes even close to rivaling the bitterness and dissatisfaction of these epigrams is Smith's letters to George Sterling, many of which were written around the time of his *Auburn Journal* column. In later years (the 1930s and beyond), at least to judge from his other letters, Smith became more even-tempered and even-handed in his reactions to his acquaintances, to Auburn, to people in general. Or perhaps he simply became more resigned. In any event, *The Devil's Notebook* is invaluable for giving us this nearly unprecedented glimpse of an earlier Smith, one in whom—for all that he was approaching thirty at the time—the youthful fires and intolerances were still burning very brightly.

Smith's targets are many; most of them he hits square-on. Here are a few of the subjects on which Smith is not reluctant to share an opinion: modern poetry ("Vers librist: a Bolshevik trying to start something in Parnassus"); utility vs. value ("It does not follow that onions are superior to narcissi, because they happen to be edible"—surely aimed at his "get-a-job" critics); his anti-intellectual stance ("Philosopher: A victim of thought who mistakes the disease for the remedy, and failing to cure himself, sets out to inoculate others"); the New Politics ("Socialist: one who believes that tigers should go halves with jackals"). The wickedest barbs are reserved for gossip, propriety, and the provincial mentality: one senses that these particular epigrams were Smith's way of taking revenge on Auburn for being Auburn ("Small town snobbery: the cutworm putting on airs when it meets the potato-bug"). One also senses that a subset of epigrams flaunt Smith's amorous affairs with Auburn's housewives[148]—we are given numerous meditations on the subjects of rouge and shoulder straps, for instance.

And what a critical luxury (for someone who did a lot of synopsifying for the Smith *Reader's Guide*) to be able to quote some favorite pieces from this collection *in full*!

Morality: the theory that nature went wrong in creating women with legs.
The ascetic and the sensualist are animated by the same illusion. One through denial, the other through indulgence, dreams that he can escape from himself.
Dance: a device for determining in public just how far it is safe to go in private.
How delightful to be a priest! So many things are forbidden to priests!
One can always learn something from adversity and misfortune. One can at least learn the world's inhumanity.

As we see, Smith by turns sugared his pronouncements with humor, glazed them with sarcasm, or left their scornful taste untouched. We can appreciate them as scholars with an interest in Smith's life and thought; and we can react to them as opinionated individuals ourselves, while holding in mind and heart an observation by Don Herron that couldn't be more true: that "these collected epigrams would not honestly deserve his title *The Devil's Notebook* if they left everyone unoffended."

---

148. The real details of this situation are not known to me—I can only hope that Smith scholarship will shortly pursue this significant subject!

CHAPTER FIFTEEN
CLARK ASHTON SMITH: COSMICIST OR MISANTHROPE?

In his Foreword to Clark Ashton Smith's literary notebook, *The Black Book*,[149] Marvin R. Heimstra uses the word "cosmic" six times in the course of three brief paragraphs, to describe Smith's literary inclinations and philosophical point of view. Mr. Heimstra is not alone in his choice of words: over the years, many critics and reviewers have labeled either Smith or his artistry with exactly this term. It may be, though, that we have an instance here of something more "said" than "true". Could it be that the critics have consistently misheard Smith's voice? In Clark Ashton Smith's writings, is it cosmicism or misanthropy that speaks the loudest?

First, what do we mean by a "cosmic" story (or poem or play)? By even posing this question we tend to be playing H. P. Lovecraft's game: he popularized the term, and in so doing put his finger on the most powerful and distinctive quality of his own work. Taking the lead from Lovecraft, I would say that such works are associated with concepts vast and vastly mysterious, and with the use of startling, unearthly imagery;[150] they partake of a distant perspective, and above all are pervaded with an *indifference* toward human affairs, thus provoking a sense of

---

149. *Black Book of Clark Ashton Smith* (Sauk City WI: Arkham House, 1979.)

150. Dreams provided this sort of imagery for some writers, Lovecraft and Donald Wanderi being two examples.

our littleness and transience. We must be quick to point out that cosmicism cannot simply be equated with the qualities of fiction on the grand scale (an association that would make bedfellows of Lovecraft's "Call of Cthulhu" and Doc Smith's *Planet-Breaker*): a cosmic work need not be vast in scale, but can instead be vast in its implications, by invoking gulfs lying unsuspected beyond daily life. A list of writers who have chosen to work from time to time in this arena would include Olaf Stapledon, William Hope Hodgson, Donald Wandrei, Lovecraft, T. E. D. Klein. Lovecraft himself would add Machen and Blackwood to the list, and exclude Lord Dunsany.

In the above description of the qualities that seem to characterize cosmicism, the words "unsuspected" and "mysterious" are telling. Both point to the same thing—to mankind's essential ignorance of the true nature of things. The cosmos is mysterious because mankind is ignorant; mankind is ignorant because mankind is small. But for what is to follow, it is extremely important to understand that *this does not constitute a judgment against humanity, but rather a realization of the immensity, the* inhumanity *of the cosmos*; as we would expect, the focus of the statement is not on mankind but on the vastness of the impersonal universe.

And this brings us to Clark Ashton Smith because, for all that he was many things, he was never an indifferent watcher of humanity. Smith's attitude was quite hostile toward humanity as a whole, and herein lies one of two focal points for an understanding of his alleged "cosmicism". Into Smith's hostility, many have read indifference; and this, together with his Romantic penchant for describing events at the grand scale -and there is no grander scale than the astronomical - has led Smith's readers to proclaim his distant, "cosmic" viewpoint. (It is worth mentioning in passing that, for some readers, Smith has simply been carried into the "cosmic" category on Lovecraft's coat-tails.) Below, I discuss individually these two tendencies, towards misanthropy and Romanticism, that taken together give Smith the appearance of an author who writes from a distant perspective.

The temperamental gulf separating the poet Smith from his Auburn neighbors was immense. As one critic has noted, Smith's delicate verse, or his translations from the French of Baudelaire, were likely to find themselves in *The Auburn Journal* "on the same page as an ad for Cohen's July clearance of muslin undergarments";[151] one of his stories groups poets of Romantic inclinations together with "double-headed snakes [and] five-legged calves".[152] Smith's sense of isolation bred hostility, and his early letters to George Sterling literally bristle with hatred for his more mundane fellows. With time, the scope of his disdain widened, and at one point he called human beings "the stupidest, greediest and most cruel of the fauna on this particular planet"[153]. No distant judgment, that!

Smith himself recognized the core of misanthropy (the recent reminiscences of a friend[154] reveal that Smith avoided all restaurants save empty ones) that gave rise to his hostile attitude and his "personal disenchantment with the social world"[155]: in a reflective letter to Lovecraft, he likened himself poignantly to Randolph Carter in Lovecraft's "The Silver Key", who seeks to abandon the present-day world and regain his pleasant childhood. "With me, though," he said, "there is no conscious desire to go back in time-only a wild aspiration toward the unknown, the uncharted, the exotic...."[156]

---

151. Hal Rubin, "Clark Ashton Smith—Ill-Fated Master of Fantasy" in *Sierra Heritage*, June 1985.

152. *The Monster of the Prophecy* (West Warwick RI: Necronomicon Press, 1988).

153. Letter to Robert H. Barlow, 16 May 1937; reprinted in *Klarkash-Ton: The Journal Of Smith Studies* #1 (Cryptic Publications, 1988).

154. Robert B. Elder, interviewed by Henry Vester in *Fungi* #6 (Summer 1985).

155. Letter to H. P. Lovecraft, ca. 24 October 1930 (Letter #15 In *Clark Ashton Smith: Letters to H. P. Lovecraft* [West Warwick RI: Necronomicon Press, 1987]).

156. *Ibid.*

It was through fiction-writing and versifying that Smith sought his refuge, his "escape from the human aquarium".[157] In his short stories, the fictional worlds Smith created are often more anti-human than non-human (the distinction is epitomized by "Marooned in Andromeda",[158] in which a voyager to an alien planet is swallowed by a carnivorous plant and is promptly spat out as unpalatable). He portrayed humanity less as an inconsequential bacterium against the immense backdrop of the universe, than as a pestilential virus. His story synopses provide the most succinct statements of intent, and here we see his acerbity and hostile point of view in their undiluted forms. A classic example is "Masters of the Dark Mountain"[159], in which terrestrial voyagers to Pluto are tested by "highly evolved beings... with a view to learning whether any relationship with terrestrials is desirable. Following the test, the Masters decide in the negative". In "The Forgotten Beast"[160], the last man on Earth is "regarded with aesthetic horror" by Earth's inheritors; and similarly treated are the colonists in "The After-Men",[161] who return to the Earth after ages have passed and find themselves "regarded with horror, treated as monsters" by the sophisticated creatures that now dominate the planet. In "The Destination of Gideon Balcoth"[162] a London businessman is abducted by aliens and whisked to their home world, to serve "as ocular proof that anything so unnatural and bizarre as humanity could exist". And in the completed story "The Seven Geases"[163] the pompous and bellicose Ralibar Vooz, toward whom Smith is hostile as an

---

157. Letter to Lovecraft, ca. 27 January 1931 (letter #20 in *Letters to H. P. Lovecraft*)

158. *Other Dimensions* (Sauk City WI: Arkham House, 1970).

159. *The Black Book*, item 16.

160. *Ibid.*, item 8.

161. *Strange Shadows: The Uncollected Fiction and Essays of Clark Ashton Smith* (Westport CT: Greenwood Press, 1989).

162. *Ibid.*

163. *Lost Worlds* (Sauk City WI: Arkham House, 1944).

individual, is told by a member of an advanced race of serpent-scientists that our species represents "a very uncouth and aberrant life-form". Clearly, Smith's misanthropy extended into his literary output.[164]

The second ingredient contributing to the perception of cosmicism in Smith's work is the epic and astronomical scale of many of his productions, both in poetry and prose. The astronomical universe was a place of grandiose beauty and powerful drama for Clark Ashton Smith, and he felt drawn to write of it: "To my imagination, [nothing] seems half so portentous as the going-out of a sun. I admit that I have been, and still am, obsessed by visions of stupendous dooms"[165] When we read his poetic sagas of the sun, the wandering stars, comets, the abyss, it's natural for us to conclude that Smith's perspective is a cosmic one. But with closer scrutiny, we see that the approach Smith took with his versifying was classical and Romantic: forces and objects are personified, comets sing "songs" of their travels, etc. This sort of sentimentality is entirely at odds with a truly detached, cosmic outlook.

I must admit that I do find it difficult to reconcile the above arguments against cosmicism in Smith with some of his own occasional statements of his viewpoint. He did, truth to tell, pen the following: "Science, philosophy, psychology, humanism, after all, are only candle-flares in the face of the eternal night with its infinite reserves of strangeness, terror, sublimity".[166] This could serve as the very motto and creed of cosmicism. And

---

164. In fairness to Smith, we should exercise some caution before treating some of his fictions as representing a misanthropic, anti-human world-view, for it is probably true to some extent that they also reflect a reaction against the narrow-minded humanism of the yarns being published at the time in, say, *Wonder Stories*. But I feel that enough examples could be taken from his fiction, poetry. and correspondence (both published and unpublished) to confirm beyond question his innate hostility towards humanity.

165. Letter to George Sterling, 11 September 1912.

166. Letter to Lovecraft, ca. Early October 1930 (Letter #13 in *Letters to H. P Lovecraft*).

in a letter from 1930 he lamented that "there are not many people with a sense of the cosmic strangeness and mystery".[167] But these statements notwithstanding, the bottom line is that Smith rarely endowed his productions with a sense of the cosmic. Even in a story like the aborted "Vizaphmal in Ophiuchus",[168] a story he looked forward to writing because it would "not bring in any human characters it all"[169] the characters and events Smith envisioned for it were all tediously mundane and 'human'[170]. I cannot account for this disparity between intent and result: perhaps Smith found the technical difficulties of maintaining reader identification and interest in the "cosmic" brand of story too daunting. Or perhaps Smiths definition of "cosmic" simply does not coincide with my own.

But now let me step back and in essence retract some of what I have said. While I do feel that the bulk of Smith's alleged cosmicism is a misinterpretation, he *was* capable on occasion of writing from a cosmic viewpoint unsoiled by derision and hostility. I find hints of the intrusion of the truly cosmic in several of Smith's productions: the mysterious classic "City of the Singing Flame" and the similar "Secret of the Cairn" (published as "The Light from beyond"—though in both we find the taint of an unwanted classicism, viz. the "Siren" motif of the first and the "Tree of Life" imagery of the second), "Master of the Asteroid", the concluding paragraph of "The Beast of Averoigne", perhaps others; at this point, of course, we are dealing with fine and subjective distinctions.

To summarize my own overall belief: what we have come to think of as cosmicism in Clark Ashton Smith is in fact some-

---

167. Letter to Lovecraft, ca. 24 October 1930 (Letter #15 in *Letters to H. P Lovecraft*).

168. *Strange Shadows*.

169. Letter to Lovecraft, ca. 16 November 1930 (Letter #17 in *Letters to H. P Lovecraft*).

170. The same failing is demonstrated by the various gods and demons that Smith created for his fictions; all, regrettably, are "human" in their behavior and inclinations.

thing else, something that arose from the combined influences of two aspects of Smith's personality, the Romantic and the misanthrope. They together manage to give the appearance of a cosmic perspective in much of his fiction and poetry, but it is largely an appearance only. In short, for the true cosmicist Lovecraft, there was the immensity of the physical universe, while for Clark Ashton Smith, the sense of distance and isolation from his fellow men.

CHAPTER SIXTEEN
CLARK ASHTON SMITH: VIRGIN? A LETTER FROM RAINE BENNETT TO H. L. MENCKEN

Introductory Note by Steve Behrends

The cherry-snows are falling now...
Brief as the snow their stainless white.
—from Smith's "The Cherry-Snows"

The mists of time veil many things. Most things, really, when you stop to think about it. Without doubt they conceal, in with all the rest, the day Clark Ashton Smith awoke as a virgin and retired otherwise; we know nothing whatever about it.

Yet for all that this hidden day must have dawned—it has for man nearly the certainty of death or taxes—I can scarcely conceive of it. Clark Ashton Smith, a virgin, ever, at any time? Surely, Smith could only have entered this world as he left it, randy and experienced. This man, this iconoclast, this poet, this Don Juan of the foothills, this John-John Kennedy of the hermit/literati set, was a womanizer of the first water. "If you know any superfluous virgins," he requests of poet George Sterling, "you might give them my address. But tell them to bring enough money for return fare!"[171] This wholesome senti-

---

171. CAS to George Sterling, 15 March 1925 (ms., New York Public Library). My thanks to Doug Anderson for providing information on this correspondence.

ment echoes further in his dictum: "I never make love to girls. 'Only married women need apply.'"[172]

To hear Smith tell it, his successes were legion. That sententious, cadenced voice we experience in "The Elder Tapes," positively thrilling in its grandeur, was wont to whisper duplicitous nothings into the ears of countless housewives. (And how could they be expected to resist the amorous advances of the local sleepy-eyed poet, when their husbands all sold auto insurance?) They hung like trophies on the wall of Smith's mind: "I had a dull time during the holidays (everybody's husband was home, not to mention the children!)."[173] And in the fullness of time, each departed that wall without ceremony: "I haven't seen my ladyfriend...for some time: she's had her father on her hands for the past fortnight. Methinks I'll begin hunting for an orphan!"[174]

Virgin Smith? Again, the mind rebels. Was there ever a time of innocence for the creator of "Ripe Mulberries"?

> Under the spreading mulberry tree
> When the purple fruit was falling free,
> I got horny and had some nooky
> With my hot cookie
> And she had some with me.[175]

Or for the poet of "The Temptation"?

> One, with deft lascivious fingers
> Holds the soft and coral chalice
> Of her rounded vulva gaping
> For the horizontal phallus.[176]

---

172. CAS to George Sterling, 31 January 1921.

173. CAS to Sterling, 3 January 1923.

174. CAS to George Sterling, 10 May 1923.

175. *Strange Shadows* (1989).

176. Unpublished.

Hyperbole aside, Smith must surely have lived as a virgin for nearly two decades; but I am equally sure that he viewed this period as a profound waste of time. He expresses this viewpoint incontrovertibly in his fiction. Given the number of stories he composed—over 100—and the concomitant crop of characters he created—300?—400?—chance alone would dictate that some number of these should be inexperienced in the ways of love. But few of them are happy. The only happy virgins I can think of in all of Smith's fiction are those two oddballs from "The Witchcraft of Ulua", Sabmon and Amalzain. Sabmon dwells in a hut of bones; this alone explains his condition, if not his attitude. Amalzain wishes only to study his algebra; I find I can add nothing whatever to that.

But enough. Let us turn now to the dark days before Smith's deflowering. Thanks to the researches of S. T. Joshi, that inveterate Blower of the Mists of Time, we have been given a glimpse into a might-have-been. The anecdote presented below was related by Raine Bennett to the infamous H. L. Mencken. Of Raine Bennett I know very little; from his letter to Mencken we gather he was part of the San Francisco literary set in the 1910s, and he knew both Smith and his mentor Sterling. In 1917, some years after the story told below, Bennett offered to publish Smith's second poetry collection—this would have been *Ebony and Crystal*—gratis,[177] but nothing ever came of it.

Bennett tells us he met Smith on the poet's first visit to San Francisco, aet. seventeen. We think he is a little off, here: Smith had not started corresponding with Sterling, his host in S.F. and environs, until after his eighteenth birthday. He paid a long visit to Sterling, perhaps his first, in June 1912 when he was nineteen; this was perhaps the time of Bennett's meeting.

This anecdote, you'll find, is a fine chuckle. The misfire described therein, Smith was to correct at some later, unknown date. One month after the long visit to S.F. and Carmel, Smith complained to Sterling, "I'd have a better chance with the girls

---

177. CAS to George Sterling, 3 March 1917.

of the place [Auburn] if I weren't such a pariah."[178] Was this a virgin's lonely whimper, or possibly the frustrated whine of a fellow who has had a taste and wants more? Had dear old George Sterling persisted in his endeavors, and succeeded where Bennett failed? Again, those mists.

In closing, my mind is drawn to an epigram of The Poet Smith. It argues that the only difference between hyenas and biographers—or snoopy critics in general—is that hyenas don't write.

—Steve Behrends

THE LETTER

Room 1438,
George Washington Hotel,
New York 10, N.Y.
26 November 1950

Mr. H. L. Mencken,
Baltimore, Md.

Dear Mr. Mencken:

This being a quiet Sunday following what the papers describe as one of Manhattan's "worst gales in history" I have indulged in a favorite indoor sport: browsing through the books of my choice. At the moment, I have finished a succulent chapter in your Newspaper Days entitled "A Girl From Red Lion, P.A."[179]

---

178. CAS to George Sterling, 4 August 1912.

179. H. L. Mencken, "A Girl from Red Lion, P.A.", *Newspaper Days 1899-1906* (New York: Knopf, 1941), pp. 227-38. The story concerns an innocent-looking young woman who arrives in Baltimore and asks a taxi driver to take her to a "house of ill repute." The taxi driver, startled by the request, grudgingly takes her to a high-class whorehouse, where the young woman tells the madam that she is a farm girl from Red Lion, Pennsylvania, who has

It recalls an experience, with a few similarities, which the late George Sterling and I had in San Francisco some years ago. Thinking it might amuse you now, I am moved to put it down on paper:

At the time, I was publishing a little art magazine called *Bohemia* which relied upon local talent for its stories, verses and drawings. Sterling was an occasional contributor. Moreover, he used to round up promising recruits. And so it happened one day that he brought a young man into the editorial cell who had just arrived—not from Red Lion, P.A., but from Auburn, California. George introduced him as Clark Ashton Smith. Verging on 17,[180] he wrote precocious rather than atrocious poetry, and had recently achieved publication as the author of "Nero,"[181] hailed by a few discerning San Franciscans as comparable to "Thanatopsis" which Bryant wrote, I believe, when around the same age.

My office, then, was on the upstairs corner of Commercial and Montgomery streets where, not long before, a madame and her five girls had been dispossessed—not because of their social activities, but because patronage had not been brisk enough to pay the rent. So our quarters were garish, and Bohemia flourished amid the ruins until our own patronage dealt us a similar fate.

After introducing Clark Ashton Smith, George asked if he

---

fallen in love with a local boy named Elmer and slept with him; but she now feels (after having read many romance novels given to her by Elmer) that she has lost her good name and, in the manner of romance heroines, must go to the city, lead a life of shame, and die in the gutter. She has resolutely set out on this course of action, but Mencken and a colleague—whom the madam summoned to hear the story—persuade the young woman that her transgression was very slight and she should go home. (Note by S. T. Joshi)

180. Smith was probably nineteen at this time, as his first visit to San Francisco with Sterling dates to the summer of 1912.

181. "Nero" was first published in *The Star-Treader and Other Poems* (1912), although some lines of it had appeared previously in various San Francisco newspapers as a result of George Sterling's championing of the poem. (Note by S. T. Joshi)

would be good enough to wait in one of the rear cribs (from which I had removed the bed and refurnished with a table, chairs, and Dr. Elliot's Five Foot Shelf of Books) while certain matters were discussed with me. Smith, who had never been outside of Auburn before, assented meekly and disappeared—obviously awed by one whom he regarded as his god. Then George joined me at the front desk and got down to business: "Raine, that raw kid in there is a *genius*—but he lacks an important qualification as a poet. He has never been to bed with a woman. Now, look: If he could write 'Nero' under such a handicap, can't you imagine what he might produce after he has locked hips with an inspiring Aphrodite?"

This was sound reasoning, I thought, but what could the editor of *Bohemia* do to rectify matters?

"Just this: That filly you call your 'assistant editor' might solve our problem. I know, because—well, how do you think she was able to filch that last sonnet from me for your lousy publication? So here's my proposition: When Belle comes in, explain the problem and invoke her aid. We must *humanize* that fellow. Right now, he's just a stinking virgin with a gift for phrases. Have her give him the treatment. It may result in such a flow of new poetry, in due season, that he will become known as one of America's foremost bards."

We talked it over. For Belle's sake (a Modoc Indian girl, who had taken to letters) George agreed—as a necessary precaution—to escort young Smith to a Turkish bath. Meanwhile, I was to phone the dark seductress and explain matters. I could hardly assure him of her cooperation, but we might reason with her. After all, she *had* saved a few souls in her time.

Then George called the kid forth from the rear room—where he might have been engrossed in the stanzas of Shelley—and they were gone for several hours.

Late that afternoon, Sterling and Smith returned—the latter with a fresh haircut, the down off his chin, a clean shirt and new tie. Belle had received her instructions, and agreed to the *ex cathedra* duty expected of her as an assistant editor. We introduced them, and George said to Clark: "Raine and I have to discuss the next issue with an obdurate printer, so we're going to leave you together for awhile. Take care of each other—"

Then we left for old Duncan Nicol's bar, a block away, to speculate over our drinks on what might be the outcome of a noble experiment.

We lingered for a reasonable interval, while George grew increasingly impatient. I admit, the suspense was rather trying on both of us. Unable to wait longer—about an hour had elapsed—we hightailed back to take inventory.

There they were—complacent enough, I thought, to have reached an ancient understanding. George, I am sure, was convinced that the author of "Nero" had fiddled while Belle burned, and that his protégé's future was assured. As they prepared to leave for the Bohemian Club, I asked my little Indian to remain on the excuse of a discussion about certain drawings required for the next issue. When the two poets had gone, I turned to her for a report. "What happened?" I asked.

"Gosh, Raine—*nothing* happened."

"Great Gods, why not?"

I was then to learn something myself about women:

"Well," she hesitated, "I know it was really my fault. I'm awfully sorry to have let you and George down. But the fact is, I just haven't had enough experience, I guess, to know what to do with a male virgin."

Some years have passed their grinding way. George has joined the shades, Belle has found greener pastures, and Clark Ashton Smith may have cut a few notches in his art though I have heard little about him since. It would be uncouth to assume that his inability to soar off the ground on Pegasus might be traced back to our failure; but who can say we haven't lost a successor to William Cullen Bryant? On reading your story about the gal from Red Lion, however, this little incident of my salad days was recalled, so I thought I'd pass it on *pour la sport*.

The papers, awhile ago, told of your illness. I trust you are back in stride. My native land will be the poorer, surely, when you lay down your pen.

With all best wishes,

Raine Bennett

I have no dictionary at hand in this hotel cubicle, so forgive my whimsical spelling. R.

CHAPTER SEVENTEEN
THE POET SPEAKS: A SPICED-UP CHRONOLOGY OF SMITH'S FICTION

In preparing the annotations for *Strange Shadows*, I went through copies of Smith's letters to Lovecraft, Derleth, and others, with an eye for details and anecdotes pertaining to all those fragments and synopses. Partly to amuse myself, I tried also to keep track of which stories he was working on at various times. Using this casual information, and referencing the previous work of Roy Squires and Donald Sidney-Fryer, Smith's own Log of Completed Stories (a sequential, though undated list), and some dated manuscripts in the Brown University Smith Collection, I compiled a chronology of Klarkash-Ton's prose, which included dates for his unfinished stories, and pointed out those yarns that were plotted or begun well before they *were* completed. It led off with "The Abominations of Yondo", which CAS felt to be his "first genuine weird tale", and "first published story of any value"; thus did I neglect his juvenile 'Orientales'.

Chronologies are dull affairs, of course—they can come in handy at times, but how often have you curled up with one when you wanted a fun read? It would be much more interesting, say, to have a list of the stories that the author himself considered his finest. Smith never gave us such a list; and while he *did* select his best things for inclusion in *Out of Space and Time*, he commented at the time that the "choice seems pretty difficult, since, after a few outstanding items such as 'The Double

Shadow' and 'A Night in Malnéant', I seem to find dozens or scores of fairly equal merit" (CAS to Derleth, 5 September 1941).

Still, while he may not have put them down in one place, Smith *did* have opinions about his stories, and frequently expressed them to his pen-pals. In an effort to bridge the gap between arid scholarship and light entertainment, some of these comments have been gathered together, along with other informational tidbits, and appear below the pertinent title in the following, 'spiced-up' Smith chronology. (Due to the large number of quotations, I haven't tried to list the letters in which they appear.)

A date in brackets indicates a date of completion, unless noted; and a number in parenthesis before a title gives that story's place in Smith's Completed Stories log. This ordering has been followed as much as possible, despite minor disagreements with dates from other sources. Only when a tale's completion was considerably delayed with respect to its inclusion in the log, has the ordering been changed. Unfinished works are marked with an asterix.

"The Abominations of Yondo" [1925] "I think it was mainly Lovecraft's interest and encouragement that led me to ['Yondo'], which appeared in *The Overland Monthly*" and "evok[ed], I was told, many protests from the readers".

(1) "Sadastor" [1925]

(2) "The Ninth Skeleton" [after 4/28 and before 8/28]

(3) "The Last Incantation" [10/23/29]

"The End of the Story" [10/1/29] "It's a good tale—especially from the sales-angle".

(4) "The Phantoms of the Fire" [10/6/29] "I prefer nearly all my other tales".

(5) "A Night in Malnéant" [10/15/29] "One of my best atmospherics".

(6) "The Resurrection of the Rattlesnake" [10/10/29] "Pretty punk, except for the touch of genuine horror at the end".

"There isn't much to it".
- (7) "Thirteen Phantasms" [10/11/29]
- (8) "The Venus of Azombeii" [11/11/29] "A weird mixture of poetry and melodrama".
- (9) "The Tale of Satampra Zeiros" [11/16/29] "One of my best".
- (10) "The Monster of the Prophecy" [12/3/29] "One of my favorite yarns". "Absolutely novel in inter-planetary fiction". "The result of a definite inspiration". "The plot ...was good from any angle; and I am willing to bet that the satiric implications will be missed by a lot of readers". "I'm sure it's the first interplanetary story on record, where the hero doesn't return to earth at the end!"
- (11) "The Metamorphosis of Earth" [late 1929] "Based on a far from bad idea". "Probably the best element is the satire". "... Am now engaged in killing off an odious bunch of scientists...."
- (12) "The Epiphany of Death" [1/25/30] "Inspired by 'Randolph Carter' and...written in about three hours".
- (13) "A Murder in the Fourth Dimension" [1/30/30]
- (14) "The Parrot in the Pawn-Shop" [1/5/30]
- (15) "A Copy of Burns" [2/27/30]
- (16) "The Devotee of Evil" [3/9/30]
- (17) "The Satyr" [1/31/30]
- (18) "The Planet of the Dead" [4/6/30]
- (19) "The Uncharted Isle" [4/21/30]
- * "Vizaphmal in Ophiuchus" [plotted 4/30]
- (20) "Marooned in Andromeda" [5/16/30, begun 1/24/30] "An excellent peg for a lot of fantasy, horror, grotesquery and satire".
- (21) "The Root of Ampoi" [5 /28/30] "A dud".
- (22) "The Necromantic Tale" [6/23/30]
- (23) "The Immeasurable Horror" [7/13/30]
- (24) "A Voyage to Sfanomoë" [7/17/30] "A sort of favorite with me". He listed it among his best pseudo-scientific yarns.
- (25) "The Door to Saturn" [7/26/30] "This tale is one of my favorites, partly on account of its literary style". "I take out

the ms. and read it over, when I am too bored to read anything in my book-cases!"
(26) "The Red World of Polaris" [late 8/30] "Passably written, but suffer[ing] from triteness of plot". "It was written on several mountain-tops, beneath the thousand-year-old junipers on granite crags; and the giant firs and hemlocks by the margin of sapphire tarns". "Mere words didn't seem to stand up in the presence of those peaks and cliffs. But now, amid the perspective of familiar surroundings, 'The Red World' doesn't seem so bad".
(27) "Told in the Desert" [?]
(28) "The Willow Landscape" [9/8/30]
(29) "A Rendezvous in Averoigne" [9/13/30] "One of my own favorites—in fact, I like it much better than the celebrated 'End of the Story'".
* "The Eggs From Saturn" [begun late 9/30] "[will feature] a realistic local setting for its interplanetary mysteries and horrors".
* "The Ocean-World of Alioth" [plotted and begun late 9/30]
(30) "The Gorgon" [10/2/30]
(31) "An Offering to the Moon" [10/30] "No great favorite of mine". "Maybe I tried too much for character-study and contrast, to the detriment of the weird atmosphere and the 'action'".
(32) "The Kiss of Zoraida" [10/15/30] "An ungodly piece of pseudo-Oriental junk". "Well enough done, with some touches of terrific irony".
(33) "The Face by the River" [10/30]
(34) "Like Mohammed's Tomb" [10/30]
* "The Sorceress of Averoigne" [plotted late 10/30]
(35) "Checkmate" [11/7/30]
(36) "The Ghoul" [11/12/30] "The legend is so hideous, that I would not be surprised if there were some mention of it in the *Necronomicon*".
(37) "A Tale of Sir John Maundeville" [11/16/30] "A good short". "['Sir John' and The Ghoul'] pleased me for their archaism".

"The kingdom of Antchar, which I have invented for this tale, is even more unwholesome, if possible, than Averoigne".
(38) "An Adventure in Futurity" [12/27/30] "An awful piece of junk".
(39) "The Justice of the Elephant" [12/29/30]
(40) "The Return of the Sorcerer" [1/6/31] An "original plot; but it seems to need some additional atmospheric development".
(41) "The City of the Singing Flame" [1/15/31] "Some day I must look for those two boulders.... If you and other correspondents cease to hear from me, you can surmise what has happened!"
* "A Tale of Gnydron" [plotted 2/31] Note: Zothique conceived.
(42) "A Good Embalmer" [2/7/31] "Have spent three days over a six-page horror... It is not in my natural genre, and may not even have the dubious merit of being salable". "[It] should take the palm for macabre grotesquery".
(43) "The Testament of Athammaus" [1/22/31, plotted 4/30] "I shall feel rather peeved if Wright turns it down; since it is about as good as I can do in the line of unearthly horror". "I really think he (or it) is about my best monster to date".
(44) "The Amazing Planet (A Captivity in Serpens)" [3/31, begun 11/30] "I'll give them their 'action' this time!!!"
(45) "The Letter from Mohaun Los" [4/9/31]
(46) "The Hunters from Beyond" [4/28/31] "I'm none too fond of the story". "Doesn't please me very well—the integral mood seems a little second-rate, probably because the modern treatment is rather uncongenial for me".
(47) "The Holiness of Azédarac" [5/21/31] "The plot maketh rather a merrie tale, methinks".
(48) "The Maker of Gargoyles" [6/16/31]
(49) "Beyond the Singing Flame" [6/30/31] "Strikes me as the best thing I have done recently".
(50) "Seedling of Mars (The Martian)" [7/20/31] "A pretty fair scientifictional opus".
* "The Master of Destruction" [plotted 8/31] "It ought to make

a thriller".

(51) "The Vaults of Yoh-Vombis" [9/12/31] "A rather ambitious hunk of extra-planetary weirdness". "The interplanetary angle...adds considerably to the interest". In October 1932 Smith submitted "Yoh-Vombis" (and "Empire of the Necromancers") to an anthologist, as examples of his best work.

* "The Rebirth of the Flame" [plotted before 9/22/31]

(52) "The Eternal World" [9/27/31] "The best and most original of my super-scientific tales, so far". "The toughest job I have ever attempted". "Gernsback took 'The Eternal World,' but advised me to put 'more realism' into my future stories, saying that the late ones were 'verging dangerously on the weird.' That's really quite a josh—as well as a compliment".

(53) "The Demon of the Flower" [10/17/31] Smith had considered including this in *The Double Shadow*, as one of his best stories not sold to magazines".

* "Slaves of the Black Pillar" [plotted and begun 10/31]

(54) "The Nameless Offspring" [11/12/31, plotted 1/31] "The plot is about as diabolic as anything I am ever likely to devise". This work was inspired by Arthur Machen's "The Great God Pan".

(55) "A Vintage from Atlantis" [11/31] "It is far from bad".

(56) "The Weird of Avoosl Wuthoqquan" [11/25/31]

(57) "The Invisible City" [12/15/31] "A hunk of tripe.... Not enough atmosphere to make it good—and too many unexplained mysteries for the scientifiction readers, who simply must have their formulae ...am pretty thoroughly disgusted by it". "So punk that I don't want to show it to anyone".

(58) "The Immortals of Mercury" [1/19/32] "A lot of tripe, I'm afraid; but if it brings me a 200.00 dollar check, will have served its purpose".

(59) "The Empire of the Necromancers" [1/7/32] "A tale which pleased me considerably". "There is a queer mood in this little tale...it is much over-greened with what [Lovecraft] once referred to as the 'verdigris of decadence.'"

(60) "The Seed from the Sepulcher" [2/32] "[I like it] for its imaginative touches, but am going to chuck the malignant plant idea after this. I don't want to run it into the ground!"

(61) "The Second Interment" [1/29/32]

(62) "Ubbo-Sathla" [2/15/32]

(63) "The Double Shadow" [3/14/32]

(64) "The Plutonian Drug" [4/5/32] "Among my best in the field of science-fiction". "It was certainly tough writing, and I'm still a little groggy". "Hellishly hard to do".

(65) "The Supernumerary Corpse" [4/10/32, plotted 11/30]

(66) "The Master of the Asteroid" [6/9/32]

(67) "The Colossus of Ylourgne" [5/1/32] "Others have commended the tale, so I begin to think that perhaps I have under-estimated it". "[It has a] striking plot".

(68) "The Mandrakes" [5/15/32] "Not a very important item".

(69) "The Beast of Averoigne" [6/18/32] "Rather good—terse, grim, and devilishly horrible". "I think that I have done better tales, but few that are technically superior".

(70) "A Star-Change" [6/32, plotted 10/30] "A whale of an idea". "A high-grade science-fiction tale". "'A Star-Change' is more realistic [than 'The Light from Beyond'], but, in my estimation, is equally good. As far as I know it is the only attempt to convey the profound disturbance of function and sensation that would inevitably be experienced by a human being on an alien world".

(71) "The Disinterment of Venus" [7/32, plotted 6/31] "A rather unimportant piece". "This, of all my recent tales, will be hardest to sell, since it combines the risque and the ghastly". "Rather a wicked story".

(72) "The White Sybil" [7/14/32]

(73) "The Ice-Demon" [7/22/32] "Well written. But I had to work it over so much that it went stale on me, somehow".

(74) "The Isle of the Torturers" [7/31/32] "The best of the summer's crop...a strange mixture of eeriness, grotesquery, bright color, cruelty, and stark human tragedy". "One of my own favorites".

(75) "The Dimension of Chance" [8/32] "Probably better as a satire than anything else".

(76) "The Dweller in the Gulf" [8/32] Smith had bad luck with this story. He considered it "a first-rate interplanetary horror, sans the hokum of pseudo-explanation", and yet to sell it on second submission he was forced to add a character (John Chalmers) to provide just such "hokum". "The tale has a magnificent Dantesque ending", which was hacked apart by Hugo Gernsback himself when it appeared in *Wonder Stories*.

(77) "The Maze of Maal Dweb" [9/32] "Ultra-fantastic, full-hued and ingenious, with an extra twist or two in the tail for luck". The title was originally "The Maze of Mool Dweb", but Smith felt that "Maal Dweb—two syllables—would be preferable perhaps, for tone-color, etc". After finalizing this title, he indulged in a bit of self-praise: "I think it should be admitted that some of my nomenclature achieves certain nuances of suggestive and atmospheric associative value".

(78) "The Third Episode of Vathek" [9/16/32] "I really think the ending is one of the best pieces of work I have done lately".

(79) "Genius Loci" [9/26/32] "An experiment for me.... It was damnably hard to do, and I am not certain of my success. I am even less certain of being able to sell it to any editor—it will be too subtle for the pulps, and the high-brows won't like the supernatural element".

(80) "The Light from Beyond" [10/31/32, plotted 8/31] "First-rate".

(81) "The Charnal God" [11/15/32] "A devil of a yarn—necromancy, invultuation, necrophilism and necrophagy—but strictly moral at the end, since the foul necromancers get it in the neck". "For my taste, it has a little too much plot and not enough atmosphere".

(82) "The Dark Eidolon" [12/23/32] "A devil of a story, and if Wright knows his mandrakes, he certainly ought to take it on. If the thing could ever be filmed...it might be a winner for diabolic drama and infernal spectacles". "Contains some

of my best imaginative writing".

(83) "The Voyage of King Euvoran" [1/33]

(84) "Vulthoom" [2/14/33, begun 10/32] "Fails to please me". "[It] seems to have pleased [Wright] for some ungodly reason; but after all it's a cut or two above Edmond Hamilton".

(85) "The Weaver in the Vault" [3/14/33] "I like the tale myself, particularly some of the atmospheric touches".

(90)* "The Infernal Star" [begun early 3/33]

(86) "The Flower-Women" [3/33, begun 10/32]

(87) "The Dark Age" [4/33] "My lousiest in many moons, largely no doubt, because of the non-fantastic plot, which failed to engage my interest at any point. The one redeeming feature is the final paragraph, which takes a sly, underhanded crack at the benefits (?) of science".

(89) "The Death of Malygris" [4/33]

(91) "The Tomb-Spawn" [begun 7/33]

* "The House of Haon-Dor" [begun 7/33]

(92) "The Witchcraft of Ulua" [8/22/33] "I feel that it is well-written; and it gives a certain variant note to my series of tales dealing with Zothique". "Erotic imagery was employed in the tale merely to achieve a more varied sensation of weirdness". "I wouldn't have had the originality to write it a few years back".

(93) "The Coming of the White Worm" [9/15/33] "A tale that I am inclined to favour in my own estimation". "It [was] hard to do, like most of my tales, because of the peculiar and carefully maintained style and tone-colour, which involves rejection of many words, images and locutions that might ordinarily be employed in writing".

(94) "The Seven Geases" [10/1/33] "Outrageously grotesque, sardonic and satiric". "I am rather partial to that opus. These grotesque and elaborate ironies come all too naturally to me, I fear".

(88) "The Chain of Aforgomon" [1/34, begun 4/33] "A devilishly hard yarn to write.... A most infernal chore, since the original inspiration seems to have gone cold, leaving the tale

as immalleable as chilled iron".
(95) "The Primal City" [1/34]
* "The Scarlet Egg" [begun 3/34]
(96) "Xeethra" [3/21/34, plotted 8/33 or before]
(97) "The Last Heiroglyph" [4/7/34] "A whale of a weird notion".
(98)* "Shapes of Adamant" [?]
(99) "Necromancy in Naat" [2/6/35] "Seems the best of my more recently published weirds; though Wright forced me to mutilate the ending*******"
(100) "The Treader of the Dust" [2/15/35]
(101) "The Black Abbott of Puthuum" [before 4/35]
(102) "The Death of Ilalotha" [3/16/37] "Quite good, I believe, especially in style and atmosphere. It is unusually poisonous and exotic". "I seem to have slipped something over on the PTA".
(103) "Mother of Toads" [3/20/37, begun ca. 5/35] "A passable weird, with a sufficiently horrific ending".
(104) "The Garden of Adompha" [7/31/37] "A tale which I am inclined to like".
(105) "The Great God Awto" [begun9/37? (published 2/40)]
(106) "Strange Shadows" [begun 3/40? A later version, "I Am Your Shadow", may have been completed 11/41]
(107) "The Enchantress of Sylaire" [? (published 7/41)]
(108) "Double Cosmos" [3/24/40 (penultimate version), begun 3/34]
(109) "Dawn of Discord" [? (E. H. Price's rewrite published 1939 or 1940)]
(110) "House of the Monoceros" [? (Price's rewrite published 2/41)]
* "The Painter in Darkness" [begun 7/46]
"Nemesis of the Unfinished" [7/30/47 (first version)]
(111) "The Master of the Crabs" [8/3/47]
(112)* "Eviction by Night" [?]
"Morthylla" [(9 or 10)/52]
"Schizoid Creator" [(9 or 10)/52]

"Monsters in the Night" [4/11/53]
"Phoenix" [1953 (published 11/53)]
"The Theft of Thirty-Nine Girdles" [4/57, begun 10/521
"Symposium of the Gordon" [8/5/57]
"The Dart of Rasasfa" [7/21/61]

Addendum

The following synopses or incomplete stories are "major", but either cannot be dated, or have only very unrestrictive bounds on date of composition:

* "In a Hashish-Dream / A Tale of Hashish-Land" [begun in 1920s]
* "Asharia: A Tale of the Lost Planet" [plotted before 1/32] "Has great possibilities, I feel".
* "The Minotaur's Brother" [plotted after 5/26/35]
* "Offspring of the Grave" [plotted after 5/26/35]
* "I Am a Witch" [plotted after 3/16/37]
* "Mandor's Enemy" [begun in early 1950s]
* "The Wink and the Chuckle" [begun before 4/53]
* "Chincharerro" [begun after "The Wink and the Chuckle"]
* "Mnemoka" [begun in 1950s]
* "Unquiet Boundary" [begun in 1950s]
* "Djinn Without a Bottle" [begun in 1950s]
* "Beyond the Rose-Arbor" [?]
* "Maker of Prodigies" [?]
* "Music of Death" [?]
* "Queen of the Sabbath" [?]

CHAPTER EIGHTEEN
MNEMOKA by Clark Ashton Smith, completed by Steve Behrends

"I must warn you that the drug is not wholly reliable," said the drum-chested, mummy-lean keeper of the dive. His voice boomed like the croaking of some gigantic frog, that had contrived to shape itself into human vocables. "Before and after it, you must keep your mind fixed undeviatingly on whatever events you have desired to re-live. Otherwise you may re-live happenings which you have wished to forget."

"In other words, the clock is turned back? I have heard that the drug creates a complete illusion of reality—vision, hearing, taste and touch."

"Yes, as you earthmen understand illusion. When the mnemoka has taken full effect, you will have all the sensation of experiencing certain past events as if they were part of the present. There is, however, what one might call a penumbral period, varying from a half hour to a full hour, during which the past and present may intermingle or alternate, often in a very confusing manner. And sometimes the re-lived events may take a variant turn, with intervals or endings not hitherto experienced. Such variations, it would seem, are determined by hidden desires—or fears. According to our theory, this is the only way in which the past can be altered. Of course, it is all subjective... and yet there have been, in some cases, results which earthmen would hardly call subjective. Again, it is my duty to warn you... There are good reasons why the sale of mnemoka is forbidden."

"Thanks, said Space-Alley Jon, squinting upward with inexpressive eyes at Pnaglak, the gaunt Aihai who overtowered his own medium stature by a full half-yard. "You've done your duty. Now give me the drug."

The Martian's arm, long as that of a gorilla, thin as that of an age-embalmed Pharaoh, reached upward to a shelf close to the ceiling of the high, narrow vault in which he and his customer stood. He brought down a wide-bottomed vial, opaque as obsidian, with a spire-like stopper encrusted with bitumen that had run downward on the bottle itself in finger-shaped streaks before hardening.

The bitumen seal fell off in flakes under his pointed onyx-tough nails. He removed the stopper and poured the vial's contents into a small beaker standing on a tripodal table, the sole furniture of the crypt. Lifting the beaker in his leathery claws, he offered it to Jon.

"Drink the stuff quickly," he urged. "Then pay me, and go as far away from here as your legs will carry you. Users of mnemoka are not allowed to linger in the bar upstairs."

"I'll pay you first," said Jon with testy curtness. "And don't worry about my staying. I've already swilled enough of your putrid swamp-weed brandy."

With his free hand he pulled out a wallet of bright-pebbled skin that had originally formed the crop of a chameleon-bird from Venus, and tossed it, jangling harshly, on the table.

Pnaglak unzipped the wallet, took out twenty *djangas* of gold and silver alloy, and returned it.

Jon raised the beaker to his nostrils, sniffing cautiously. With senses sharpened by the perfumes and fetors of alien worlds, he could detect no odor in the thick sepia brown liquid that foamed to immense iridescent bubbles.

"Here's wishing you a bellyful of your own poisons," he toasted the proprietor, and swallowed the tasteless liquor to its last slow-oozing drops.

Before he could lower the emptied cup, it was snatched from his fingers, and the Aihai nudged him toward a flight of stairs opposite to that by which he had entered. Up steps that climbed into darkness, spaced for the gangling shins of the planet's natives, he was shooed or pushed bodily when he stumbled. As they went, the dive-keeper lapsed into the guttural Martian language that human vocal organs can hardly approximate. *"Ngrhk, grkg, grkg, ngrhk,"* he croaked in anxious objurgation.

At the top of the blind stairs, a door was opened quickly on oiled, noiseless hinges. Jon was thrust forth into a lampless alley black as the guts of an undersea fish, and the door closed behind him, its closing perceived only by a faint, sighing wafture of air.

He stood a long moment, trying to orient himself. The cold of the thin-aired night, well-nigh bitter as that of space, began to gnaw him with black teeth that pierced through his padded tunic.

The stars of Lyra's handle, swinging westward in the roof-verged chasm overhead, enabled him to regain his bearings. He followed the alley to his right, knowing that it should debouch on an esplanade along the great canal that divided Ignarh-Luth the space-port from the immemorial capitol, Ignarh-Vath. A mile eastward, on the same canal, was the Ghaggan Hotel, in which he had taken lodgings.

It was a hazardous and unsavory neighborhood, with whose doings the police concerned themselves only in some explosion of civic virtue. Here the cryptic and crafty natives pandered to the space-wandering scum of a dozen worlds and moons. Outlawed, fantastic drugs were sold, and exotic crimes and vices, older than Babylon, burgeoned darkly. .But even here it had been none too easy to find a seller of *mnemoka*, a narcotic distilled from a Martian cactus, and strictly tabooed by the Martians themselves. They would dispense it only, and then rarely, to aliens. This taboo, it seemed, was of religious origin. Some sort of vague unspecified damnation would supposedly ensue the drug's use. The stigma of necromancy was attached even to drug-dreamers who attempted to evoke the past in their dreams.

Jon had heard alluring accounts, though never at first hand, of the fabulous evocative powers of *mnemoka*. It was said that certain terrestrial addicts had been able under its influence to repeat the happiest hours of their lives, even back to infancy. As yet no earth-scientist had analyzed this narcotic, which could induce hallucinations of reality more vivid and complete than those created by any other known agent. As Pnaglak had warned, it was also tricky, and would sometimes reproduce events and effects more painful than pleasant; or would even twist the past in devious and aberrant ways. In some cases it had left stigmata such as would normally be caused only by actual physical experience.

In obedience to Pnaglak's injunction, Jon had been trying to concentrate his thoughts on the far-off episode he had consciously chosen to re-live. Rapt in this endeavor, he hastened his steps through the blind alley. There should be ample time to regain the security of his room before the drug could take its full effect. But even now he noticed a curious altering of his senses, as if the process of detachment from present realities had already begun.

The barb-tipped cold had become a little blunted, as if a premature sun had risen somewhere behind the lofty maze of buildings. In lieu of the metal-hard pavement, he seemed to be treading at times on something resilient as grass or moss. The familiar alley-stenches no longer stung his nostrils with ammoniac keenness; and through them he caught evanescent waftures of bruised mint—faint but at moments unmistakable...There was no mint anywhere on Mars. But he had lain long ago—and not alone—in a bed of mint on his natal Earth. It was that episode, removed in time by years spent on half the solar worlds, which he had wished to re-experience.

He sought to vision the face of Sophia, the young girl who had shared with him that fragrant bed. He could see her small but nubile breasts, under the lace of sunlight and willow leaf shadows; could see, could feel the warm body that had basked in the summer noon. The thrill of that yielding, virginal for both of them, remained poignant in memory. But her face returned to him with the vagueness of a reflection in moving water. Between, in brief flashes, came other faces, unbidden and unwelcome: faces of women whose venal passion or perversity he had bought—and could buy again—in many space-ports. There was no need of *mnemoka* to revive such loves as these. The price of the flame-sapphires he had sold would bring them about him in seraglios with all their languors and writhings.

With a violent effort of will, he banished the faces—and with them went the tantalizing phantom of mint, the warmth which had tempered the bleak night, the ambiguous softness beneath his feet. Once again there was nothing but the black, fetor-infested alley along which he hastened.

It was his haste, perhaps, that caused him to stumble over some unseen, heavy object. Cursing, he regained his balance and pulled out the small but powerful flash-light that he carried.

It was a man's body that had blocked his way, lying transversely, face upward, on the filthy pavement. The light played on knee-length boots and broadly belted tunic such as he himself wore—the traditional garb of space-men. The body itself might have been one of many thousands... but the face was one that he knew well, and had never thought to see again.

For an instant, Jon was aware of no horror, only the shock of a thing impossible, when his light centered upon that dead familiar face. Then came the wild hope that he was mistaken—that the man was merely someone who resembled Boris. Seeking evidence of such a mistake, he bent closer.

With sick consternation he identified the large mole above the right brow, the two identical reddish knife-scars running from jowl to eye-socket on the left cheek. The hook-nose, broken midway in its bridge, the rufous chin-beard half concealing a deep cleft, the ponderous lids above ill-matched eyes, the massively hanging under-lip—these could belong only to Boris. In further confirmation, there was the wound itself.

It could only have been caused by a soft-nosed bullet such as Jon had used, forgetting in his haste that the gun was loaded with cartridges of that type. The bullet, fired close to the right temple, had made a neat clean hole on that side. Emerging on the other, it had blown away the left ear and much of the skull and hair. Jon had regretted such messiness afterward: it had taken time to mop up the vessel's spattered wall and floor.

He had loaded the automatic with those mushroom bullets for possible use against certain rumoured Europan monsters, whose diffused vital spots could be injured little by anything less barbarous. Such monsters had remained shy and aloof during his sojourn on the moon.

And now that grisly wound, whose congealing effluent he had seen turn to crystal in the space between the worlds, was riling fresh blood that pooled darkly upon the paving. Jon accepted the unbelievable tableau before him, as one accepts the absurd horror of an oft-remembered dream, a dream whose beginning lay many months and many million miles away, when he had shot Boris with an old-type automatic kept beneath the control panel of their small space-flier, the *Pelican*, and had promptly heaved his corpse overboard in the emptiness somewhere between Europa and the asteroid belt. The two had been returning Mars-ward from Europa, after a successful season among the aborigines of that Jupiterian moon. They had traded bangles and other cheap trinkets for the gorgeous and precious flame-sapphires found in the soft marls of Europa. The simple natives, having no conception of money values, were well satisfied by such traffic. But the jewels purchased during that trip would bring them enough in Martian *djangas* to enable a middle-aged man to retire permanently from space-faring.

Weary of the vast bleak gulfs too often crossed, the bewildering alienage of outer worlds, and sick with a growing nostalgia for his native planet, Jon had planned the murder from the beginning of his partnership with Boris. They had met in a little-used, obscure port of Venus, when both had been seeking refuge from the overly inquisitive police; and on that same night started their long voyage to Europa.

No crime, it seemed, could be safer: there were few earthmen on Europa, a moon as yet uncolonized. Returning to Mars afterward, it was needless to report an accidental death for Boris, whose very existence had not been known to the authorities of that world. According to his own records, he had travelled alone. The Pelican belonged legally Jon, and Boris had left no least trace of his presence aboard the vessel.

All the evidence that might have been incriminating to him had been carefully disposed of; and now the impossible corpse of Boris lay huddled in this rank alleyway, its blood steaming as it seeped about his boots, glittering as darkly in the beam of his belt-light as had the choicest of his flame-sapphires.

At this thought, as if through some necromantic incantation, Jon found himself aboard the *Pelican*, its familiar interior spattered with fresh blood—a blood, Jon knew, that had been spilt months past; and yet he felt only a dim consternation over past and present, about that which had and that which had not been. Cool, unquestioning, the murderer looked down at the murdered; all had happened as he had planned. Two things alone remained: First, to take from Boris the pouch in which he carried his share of the flame-sapphires, which he had strapped closely to his skin. Second, to eject the corpse, together with any evidence that another person had been within the *Pelican* during that voyage.

Wasting no reflection on the ghoulishness of his job, he turned the body over, and groped beneath his partner's tunic for the pouch, which he unstrapped and then tossed to the deck. Next, he covered the bloody head with thick sacking, lifted the lifeless form, and carried it into the air-lock. He returned to the vessel's interior, and closed the air-lock's inner door behind him. His powerful arms straining at the task, he shifted the lever that unsealed the outer hatch, hearing as he did so the swish of escaping air that ejected his partner into the realm of eternal night.

* * * * * * *

He was back once more in that odor-haunted alley, standing

on an empty pavement. There was about him only the accustomed filth and offal. He recalled the warning he had been given in Pnaglak's cellar. It was all, then, an illusion brought on by the drug.

His brain and senses were clear now except for a feeling of dizziness, a humming as of a light fever in his head. Attempting to shake himself of this malaise, he walked onward, and in a moment came upon the esplanade with its brilliant but remotely spaced lamps. By its side, dark and silent, flowed the immemorial canal, ebbing slowly between slanted banks of water-scored and pitted stone; and upon its surface the reflected lamps were like fallen stars.

He thought again of Sophia—and was lying beside her, upon the wild summer-warm mint. The sun, striking her hair, bejewelled it with iridescent spangles. The rose-flushed skin between her breasts was delicately dewed with sweat. He reached out a hand to caress her. Then, abruptly, he had returned to the *Pelican*.

With old rags, and water taken from the privy, Jon knelt, cleaning the half-clotted blood from the floor. When all was to his satisfaction, he brought out from a closet the ether-suit that had belonged to Boris, together with all other articles of his clothing and personal possessions. He might have kept the suit, which had been little worn, but Boris had incised on its bosom of grey plastic the initials B.W. in crudely sprawling letters and had filled them in with an orange-red lacquer. Unzipping it, Jon stuffed all the other belongings into its legs and body, and added Boris' mess-kit and gun, and the wet, bloody rags. A minute later, it was floating in space with the corpse of its owner.

There remained the basinful of bloodied water. Jon thought of recycling it in the purifier, as was done to the water used in ablutions and all ordinary washing and cleaning. Instead, he poured it into the vessel's toilet. Anyway, there could be no shortage of water now, with himself alone for consumer.

He remembered now to set the *Pelican*'s course, locking its gears. There would be small need of vigilance before the ship reached the asteroidal zone. He took a seat on the deck beside the pouch he had taken from Boris, and spilled its contents upon the lustrous metal hull. The count of the jewels was equal to that which he himself had retained: a baker's dozen. They blazed before him, interweaving their deep blues with effulgent flames of sea-green and emerald. They were the prize of a man's life—and his own insurance against toil, poverty, and the rigors of space travel and old age.

The light of each gem flashed in his avaricious eyes, stone upon stone adding its own unique shade of indigo or emerald to the cumulative, soul-capturing glow. The jewels lay as they had fallen from the pouch, and yet their pattern captivated Jon, seeming to hold an intangible, evanescent meaning for him, like some indecipherable rune glimpsed in a book of antiquity.

As Jon stared, he became distantly aware that the emerald glow was expanding, laying a verdant patina upon the silver deck surrounding him. Only with difficulty could he see through the lambent haze to the sapphires themselves.

The misty light, such as might be seen by dwellers in ocean depths, withdrew after a moment. In the wake of its passage Jon saw before him not the gem-strewn deck of the *Pelican*, but a wildflower-scattered heath of green grass and clover, enmeshed in the tattered shadow of a willow tree. There was once again the cool scent of mint, and the lovely Sophia reclined by his side.

The sight of her soft, parted lips, and the smooth ivory of her skin, brought waves of desire pulsing through his body; his senses stirred with her nearness. Here was the light he had lost in his empty wanderings, his vain and violent pursuits. And yet, as he gazed more closely at this vision of his first love, drawn from the tombs of the past by the necromancy of the Martian drug, Jon felt the stirrings of a vague unease.

Sophia's eyes, enshrined in Jon's memory as twin pools of liquid azure, now seemed to glitter with a sapphire light; and her gaze was appraising, and without warmth. And her smile, which before had held only shyness and adoration—did he catch a hint of chill satisfaction? Despite these qualms, the blindness of his yearning drove Jon to step closer to her; but as he did so, Sophia calmly lifted her eyes to something beyond his right shoulder, as though wishing to forestall his ardour in the light of more pressing matters.

Turning, Space-Alley Jon glimpsed a man in an ether-suit a few paces behind him. Years of hateful experience stood him in good stead: he leaped to his feet, whirling into a tense crouch to face the intruder.

For a moment the figure stood unmoving, with dark visor pulled down and gloved hands at hip-level, while Jon stared in puzzlement. His opponent was of average height and seemingly stocky build, although he was unable to determine this with any certainty, for the suit configured its occupant very strangely, with many abrupt swellings and concavities along the limbs and torso. His eyes scanned further, searching for the tell-tale indications of hidden weaponry, until his gaze reached the chest of the stranger. What Jon saw there brought on a numbing of mind that rendered his many defenses useless; and the earth beneath his feet seemed to lurch with some profound dislocation. For upon that chest, lit by the warm summer sun of a year long dead, lay the deeply scored initials B. W. marked in an orange-red lacquer.

With an alien slowness the suited arm raised to the visor, bending in a boneless, fluid arc like the tentacle of a cuttlefish. The oddly bulging glove drew the visor up and back.

Jon's mind reacted sluggishly to the sight before him. "A face of smoke," he thought, "black swirls of smoke." The helmet of the ether-suit framed an oval of ebon mist, like the huge, blind eye of a Cyclops, into which the sunlight scarcely penetrated.

The gloved hand reached slowly into the helmet, disturbing its half-seen contents; and like some grey adder breaching a riven crypt, the ash-colored arm followed it over the lip of the faceplate, sliding deeper into the body of the suit. The broad chest bulged and buckled to the movements of the arm, and the initials painted upon it seemed to move rhythmically in cruel mockery of a heart's beating. As the dark shapes rustled and shifted beneath the passage of the arm, Jon dazedly realized that the void of the helmet held not smoke, but folds of a dark, wet cloth. The arm acquired great streaks of crimson as it moved among them.

After a time the sinuous member withdrew, dislodging ensanguined scraps of cloth in a foul vomit upon the grass. Held within the horribly stained glove was a glistening thing that Jon could not see clearly; and with the same unutterable langour that had characterized all its motions, the crumpled arm raised level with Jon's face.

* * * * * * *

As was the fashion of dawns in Ignarh-Luth, the paling indigo of the sky heralded a chill wind from regions beyond the Pole, heavy with the red dust of outer deserts and the grey dust of vast and ruinous cities.

Like a thing lost and suffering, the wind moaned and sighed as it scoured the deserted streets and twisted alleyways, tracing paths worn smooth by its aeons of passage. But beside the Yahan canal, whose waters still held the shadow of the night, and along the ancient esplanade, it seemed that the wind passed more quietly; and the air hardly stirred about a group of silent Aihais that had gathered at a spot by the banks.

At such an early hour, only the beggars, pariahs, and prophets of the city are on hand. Such as these stood encircling the corpse of an earthman, whose head had been shattered by a slow, heavy bullet. The copious amount of blood and other matter that should have flowed from such a devastating wound was nowhere in evidence, indicating that the death had occurred in some other locale.

Blood was found on the dead man's boots, however, in addition to the leafy sprigs of some aromatic plant, which none present could identify. There was no mint anywhere on Mars.

A NOTE ON THE STORY

"Mnemoka" was a science fiction short story that Smith attempted, but perhaps never completed, sometime in the 1950s. The 'surviving typescript' for the story in fact barely survived, having suffered significant damage in one of Smith's cabin fires. The idea of completing "Mnemoka" grew out of the frustration (felt back in 1983) of working with a Smith manuscript where, past a certain point, halves of pages of text just vanished into char—*diagonally*. Part of a sentence, a gap, then down a line and more of that sentence or the next; you get the picture, and will perceive the temptation. But of any "ending", nothing whatever remained.

Spoiler alert: I started to seriously (perhaps 'creatively' is the more generous term) fill in the gaps at about the paragraph, "And now that grisly wound..." By the point we reach "The light of each gem flashed in his avaricious eyes...", we're wholly Smith-free.

PRIMARY BIBLIOGRAPHY

In the following, (s) denotes a short story collection, (p) a poetry collection; except where noted, collections were compiled by Clark Ashton Smith. Smith's own titles for stories published under editors' titles are given in parentheses.

The Abominations of Yondo (s). Sauk City, WI: Arkham House, 1960. Contains: "The Nameless Offspring", "The Witchcraft of Ulua", "The Devotee of Evil", "The Epiphany of Death", "A Vintage from Atlantis", "The Abominations of Yondo", "The White Sybil", "The Ice Demon", "The Voyage of King Euvoran", "The Master of the Crabs", "The Enchantress of Sylaire", "The Dweller in the Gulf", "The Dark Age", "The Third Episode of Vathek" (with William Beckford), "Chinoiserie", "The Mirror in the Hall of Ebony", "The Passing of Aphrodite".

The Black Book of Clark Ashton Smith. Ed. Donald Sidney-Fryer and Rah Hoffman. Sauk City, WI: Arkham House, 1979. Smith's literary notebook. Contains synopses for stories, first drafts of poems, and epigrams; includes two memoirs by George F. Haas, "As I Remember Klarkash-Ton" and "Memories of Klarkash-Ton".

The City of the Singing Flame (s, reprint collection). Ed. Donald Sidney-Fryer. New York: Pocket/Timescape, 1981. Contains: "Poet of the Singing Flame" by Donald Sidney-Fryer, "The City of the Singing Flame" (includes "Beyond the Singing Flame"), "The White Sybil", "The Tale of Satampra Zeiros,"

"The Theft of the Thirty Nine Girdles," "The Door to Saturn," "The Dark Eidolon", "The Black Abbot of Puthuum", "The Garden of Adompha", "The Maze of Maal Dweb", "The Flower-Women", "The Enchantress of Sylaire", "The Beast of Averoigne", "The Hunters from Beyond".

Clark Ashton Smith: Letters to H. P. Lovecraft. Ed. Steve Behrends. West Warwick, RI: Necronomicon Press, 1987. Collects Smith's letters to Lovecraft from 1928-1936.

The Dark Chateau (P). Sauk City, WI: Arkham House, 1951.

The Double Shadow and Other Fantasies (s). Auburn, CA: Auburn Journal Press, 1933. Contains: "The Voyage of King Euvoran", "The Maze of the Enchanter" (later title: "The Maze of Maal Dweb"), "The Double Shadow", "A Night in Malnéant", "The Devotee of Evil", "The Willow Landscape". Texts for these stories represent unedited versions, and supercede other reprintings.

Ebony and Crystal (P). Auburn, CA: Auburn Journal Press, 1922.

The Fantastic Art of Clark Ashton Smith. Ed. Dennis Rickard, Baltimore, MD: Mirage Press, 1973. Contains black & white photographs of Smith's drawings and sculptures, with descriptions of how such work was produced.

Grotesques and Fantastiques. Ed. Gerry de la Ree, Saddle River, NJ: de la Ree, 1973. Reproduces artwork by Smith included in his correspondence with Samuel Loveman.

Genius Loci (s). Sauk City, WI: Arkham House, 1948. Contains: "Genius Loci", "The Willow Landscape", "The Ninth Skeleton", "The Phantoms of the Fire", "The Eternal World", "Vulthoom", "A Star-Change", "The Primal City", "The Disinterment of Venus", "The Colossus of Ylourgne", "The Satyr", "The Garden of Adompha", "The Charnel God", "The Black Abbot of Puthuum", "The Weaver in the Vault".

Hyperborea (s). Ed. Lin Carter. New York: Ballantine, 1971. Collects the completed Hyperborean stories, (together with "Behind the North Wind" by Lin Carter), "The Abominations of Yondo", "The Desolation of Soom" (later title: "The

Abomination of Desolation"), "The Passing of Aphrodite", "The Memnons of the Night".

In Memoriam: Clark Ashton Smith. Ed. Jack L. Chalker. Baltimore, MD: Anthem, 1963. Features articles in praise of Smith, and includes first publication of his play, "The Dead Will Cuckold You".

Klarkash-Ton and Monstro Ligriv. Ed. Gerry de la Ree. Saddle River, NJ: de la Ree, 1974. Reprints Smith's correspondence with *Weird Tales* artist Virgil Finlay.

The Last Incantation (s, reprint collection). Ed. Donald Sidney-Fryer. New York: Pocket/Timescape Books, 1982. Contains: "The Last Enchanter" by Donald Sidney-Fryer, "The Double Shadow", "The Last Incantation", "The Death of Malygris", "Seedling of Mars", "The Ice-Demon", "Ubbo-Sathla", "The Plutonian Drug", "The Colossus of Ylourgne", "The Holiness of Azédarac", "The End of the Story", "The Vaults of Yoh-Vombis", "The Devotee of Evil", "The Root of Ampoi", and "Genius Loci".

Lost Worlds (s). Sauk City, WI: Arkham House, 1944. Contains: "The Tale of Satampra Zeiros", "The Door to Saturn", "The Seven Geases", "The Coming of the White Worm", "The Last Incantation", "A Voyage to Sfanomoë", "The Death of Malygris", "The Holiness of Azédarac", "The Beast of Averoigne", "The Empire of the Necromancers", "The Isle of the Torturers", "Necromancy in Naat", "Xeethra", "The Maze of Maal Dweb", "The Flower-Women", "The Demon of the Flower", "The Plutonian Drug," "The Planet of the Dead", "The Gorgon", "The Letter from Mohaun Los", "The Light from Beyond" ("The Secret of the Cairn"), "The Hunters from Beyond", "The Theader of the Dust".

The Monster of the Prophecy (s, reprint collection). Ed. Donald Sidney-Fryer. New York: Pocket/Timescape Books, 1983. Contains: "Lyricist of Lost Worlds" by Donald Sidney-Fryer, "The Monster of the Prophecy", "Xeethra", "The Empire of the Necromancers", "The Charnel God", "The Witchcraft of Ulua", "Vulthoom," "The Weird of Avoosl Wuthoqquan",

"The Seven Geases", "The Coming of the White Worm", "(The) Master of the Asteroid", "The Immeasurable Horror", "Monsters in the Night" ("A Prophecy of Monsters"), "The Gorgon", "A Voyage to Sfanomoë".

Nostalgia of the Unknown (prose-poems, reprint collection). Eds. Marc and Susan Michaud, S.T. Joshi, and Steve Behrends. West Warwick, RI: Necronomicon Press, 1989. Reprints contents of *Poems in Prose,* together with the prose poems first published in *Strange Shadows.*

Odes and Sonnets (p, reprint collection). San Francisco: Book Club of California, 1918.

Other Dimensions (s). Ed. August Derleth. Sauk City, WI: Arkham House, 1970. Contains: "Marooned in Andromeda", "The Amazing Planet" ("A Captivity in Serpens"), "An Adventure in Futurity", "The Immeasurable Horror", "The Invisible City", "The Dimension of Chance", "The Metamorphosis of Earth", "Phoenix", "The Necromantic Tale", "The Venus of Azombeii", "The Resurrection of the Rattlesnake", "The Supernumerary Corpse", "The Mandrakes", "Thirteen Phantasms", "An Offering to the Moon", "Monsters in the Night" ("A Prophecy of Monsters"), "The Malay Krise", "The Ghost of Mohammed Din", "The Mahout", "The Raja and the Tiger", "Something New", "The Justice of the Elephant", "The Kiss of Zoraida," "A Tale of Sir John Maundeville", "The Ghoul," "Told in the Desert".

Out of Space and Time (s). Sauk City, WI: Arkham House, 1942. Contains "Clark Ashton Smith: Master of Fantasy" by August Derleth and Donald Wandrei, "The End of the Story", "A Rendezvous in Averoigne", "A Night in Malnéant", "The City of the Singing Flame" (includes "Beyond the Singing Flame"), "The Uncharted Isle", "The Second Interment", "The Double Shadow", "The Chain of Aforgomon", "The Dark Eidolon", "The Last Hieroglyph", "Sadastor", "The Death of Ilalotha", "The Return of the Sorcerer", "The Testament of Athammaus", "The Weird of Avoosl Wuthoqquan", "Ubbo-Sathla", "The Monster of the

Prophecy", "The Vaults of Yoh-Vombis", "From the Crypts of Memory", "The Shadows".

Planets and Dimensions. Ed. Charles K. Wolfe. Baltimore, MD: Mirage Press, 1973. Collects Smith's short essays from the letters-columns of the science-fiction and weird fiction magazines, together with other articles.

Poems in Prose. Ed. Donald Sidney-Fryer. Sauk City, WI: Arkham House, 1965.

Poseidonis (s). Ed. Lin Carter. New York: Ballantine, 1973. Collects the completed Atlantean stories and poems, together with "The Magic of Atlantis" by Lin Carter, "An Offering to the Moon", "The Uncharted Isle", "The Epiphany of Death", "Symposium of the Gorgon", "The Venus of Azombeii", "The Root of Ampoi", "The Invisible City", "The Willow Landscape", "The Shadows", and several poems.

A Rendezvous in Averoigne (s, reprint collection). Ed. James Turner. Sauk City, WI: Arkham House, 1988. Contains: Introduction by Ray Bradbury, "The Holiness of Azédarac", "The Colossus of Ylourgne", "The End of the Story," "A Rendezvous in Averoigne", "The Last Incantation", "The Death of Malygris", "A Voyage to Sfanomoë", "The Weird of Avoosl Wuthoqquan", "The Seven Geases", "The Tale of Satampra Zeiros", "The Coming of the White Worm", "The City of the Singing Flame", "The Dweller in the Gulf", "The Chain of Aforgomon", "Genius Loci", "The Maze of Maal Dweb", "The Vaults of Yoh-Vombis", "The Uncharted Isle", "The Planet of the Dead", "Master of the Asteroid", "The Empire of the Necromancers", "The Charnel God", "Xeethra", "The Dark Eidolon", "The Death of Ilalotha", "The Last Hieroglyph", "Necromancy in Naat", "The Garden of Adompha", "The Isle of the Torturers", "Morthylla".

Sandalwood (p). Auburn, CA: Auburn Journal Press, 1925.

Spells and Philtres (p). Sauk City, WI: Arkham House, 1958.

Selected Poems. Sauk City, WI: Arkham House, 1971.

The Star Treader and Other Poems (p). San Francisco: A. M. Robertson, 1912. Smith's first published book.

Strange Shadows: The Uncollected Fiction of Clark Ashton Smith. Ed. Steve Behrends with Donald Sidney-Fryer and Rah Hoffman. Westport, CT: Greenwood Press, 1989. Collection of fantastic and non-fantastic stories, fragments, synopses, and prose poems. Includes the completed stories "A Good Embalmer", "Double Cosmos", "Strange Shadows", "Nemesis of the Unfinished", "The Dart of Rasasfa". Reprints "The Dead Will Cuckold You".

Tales of Science and Sorcery (s). Sauk City, WI: Arkham House, 1964. Contains "Clark Ashton Smith: A Memoir" by E. Hoffmann Price, "(The) Master of the Asteroid", "The Seed from the Sepulcher", "The Root of Ampoi", "The Immortals of Mercury", "(A) Murder in the Fourth Dimension", "Seedling of Mars", "The Maker of Gargoyles", "The Great God Awto", "Mother of Toads", "The Tomb-Spawn", "Schizoid Creator", "Symposium of the Gorgon", "The Theft of (the) Thirty-Nine Girdles", "Morthylla".

The Unexpurgated Clark Ashton Smith (s). Ed. Steve Behrends. West Warwick, RI: Necronomicon Press, 1987-1988. Series of six booklets, each containing a story Smith had been forced to edit for publication. Texts are restored versions based on original manuscripts. Series contents: "The Mother of Toads", "The Dweller in the Gulf", "The Vaults of Yoh-Vombis", "The Monster of the Prophecy", "Xeethra," "The Witchcraft of Ulua".

Xiccarph (s). Ed. Lin Carter. New York: Ballantine, 1972. Contains: "Other Stars and Skies" by Lin Carter, "To the Daemon", "The Maze of Maal Dweb", "The Flower-Women", "Vulthoom", "The Dweller in the Gulf", "The Vaults of Yoh-Vombis", "The Doom of Antarion" (later title: "The Planet of the Dead"), "The Demon of the Flower", "The Monster of the Prophecy", "Sadastor", "From the Crypts of Memory".

Zothique (s). Ed. Lin Carter. New York: Ballantine, 1970. Collects the completed Zothique stories.

SECONDARY BIBLIOGRAPHY

Behrends, Steve. "The Lost Worlds of Clark Ashton Smith", Appendix I of *Strange Shadows*. Discusses the unpublished and lost weird fiction.

De Camp, L. Sprague. "Sierran Shaman: Clark Ashton Smith", Chapter VIII of *Literary Swordsmen and Sorcerers*, Sauk City, WI: Arkham House, 1974. Fact-filled and entertaining account of Smith's life, with limited criticism of the fiction and poetry.

Fryer, Donald S.: see Sidney-Fryer, Donald

Haas, George F. "As I Remember Klarkash-Ton" (IM).

___ "Memories of Klarkash-Ton". *Nyctalops* No. 8, August 1972 (Clark Ashton Smith Issue). Both articles are reprinted in BB. These two memoirs of the friendship of Haas and Smith stand as the fullest accounts of Smith's personality, mentality, and day-to-day life in his later years.

Herron, Don. "The Double Shadow". Chapter 4 of *Jack Vance*. New York: Taplinger, 1980. Notes the similar traits and characteristics in the work of Smith and Vance, including prose style, humor, satire of religion, and flair for invented names. One might also mention the common use of improbable coincidences and turns of events, as well as other *deus ex machina*, in their fiction.

Hillman, Arthur F. "The Poet of Science Fiction". *Fantasy Review* No. 14, April-May 1949. Sympathetic discussion of Smith's writing style and characteristics.

Marigny, Jean. "Clark Ashton Smith and his World of Fantasy". *Crypt of Cthulhu* No. 26 (Hallowmass 1984, Clark Ashton Smith Issue). General overview of the fiction, with emphasis on the creation of imaginary settings for story-cycles.

Rubin, Hal. "Clark Ashton Smith—Ill-fated Master of Fantasy". *Sierran Heritage, the Magazine of Placer, Nevada, El Dorado Counties*, Vol. 5. No. 1, June 1985. General discussion of Smith's life and work, featuring anecdotes related by his Auburn neighbors.

Sidney-Fryer, Donald. "The Alleged Influence of Lord Dunsany on Clark Ashton Smith". *AMRA* No. 23 (January 1963). A (rather zealous) response to L. Sprague deCamp's statement, that CAS had been influenced heavily by Dunsany's early fiction, this article constitutes a thoughtful and perceptive exposition of common trends and attitudes in Smith's work. Reprinted in *Klarkash-Ton* #1 (Cryptic Press, 1988).

___ *Emperor of Dreams*. West Kingston, RI: Donald Grant, 1978. Combination biography/bibliography featuring letters of reminiscence and appraisal from Smith's friends and contemporaries. The first book-length reference work on Smith's writings.

___ "Clark Ashton Smith, Poet in Prose". Introduction to PP.

___ "A Memoir of Timeus Gaylord". *The Romantist* No. 2, (1978). Details Fryer's visits with Clark and Carol as well as his overall involvement in Smith studies.

___ "The Sorcerer Departs" (IM). Seminal article dealing with Smith's life and work. In essence the parent of all further Smith studies.

Stockton, Richard. "An Appreciation of the Prose Works of Clark Ashton Smith". *The Acolyte*, Spring 1946. Early article of praise; emphasis on the emotional color found in CAS. Notable in that Smith felt that Stockton "really showed some understanding of my work" (letter to S. J. Sackett, 11 July 1950). Reprinted in *Klarkash-Ton* #1.

Wandrei, Donald. "The Emperor of Dreams". *The Overland Monthly and Out West Magazine*, December 1926. Praises imagination and imagery of the poetry. Rhapsodic and ecstatic, the article nearly constitutes a prose-poem itself. Reprinted in *Klarkash-Ton* #1.

Wolfe, Charles K. "CAS: A Note on the Aesthetics of Fantasy". *Nyctalops* No.8 (August 1972, Clark Ashton Smith Issue). Analysis of Smith as a writer within the Romantic tradition. Addresses Smith's reactions to the "realist" movement, including a thumbnail discussion of Smith's attitude towards illusion/reality; also notes some common tendencies in the fiction. Similar to Wolfe's equally perceptive Introduction to PD. Reprinted in *The Dark Eidolon* #2 (Necronomicon Press, 1989).

ACKNOWLEDGMENTS

"The Song of the Necromancer", first published in *Studies in Weird Fiction* #1; copyright © 1986 by Necronomicon Press

"CAS & Divers Hands", first published in *Crypt of Cthulhu* #26; copyright © 1984 by Cryptic Publications

"The Birth of Ubbo-Sathla", first published in *Crypt of Cthulhu* #45; copyright © 1987 by Cryptic Publications

"A Review of *The Devil's Notebook*", first published in *Studies in Weird Fiction* #9; copyright © 1991 by Necronomicon Press

"Clark Ashton Smith: Cosmicist or Misanthrope?", first published in *The Dark Eidolon* #2; copyright © 1989 by Cryptic Publications

"Clark Ashton Smith: Virgin?", first published in *Studies in Weird Fiction* #18; copyright © 1996 by Necronomicon Press

"The Poet Speaks", first published in *Crypt of Cthulhu* #26; copyright © 1984 by Cryptic Publications

"Mnemoka", first published in *Astro Adventures* #1; copyright © 1987 CASiana Literary Enterprises

All texts have been slightly revised for this edition.

ABOUT THE AUTHOR

STEVE BEHRENDS (b. 1959) was trained as a particle physicist, works now for MIT, and lives in the Boston area. He is the author of several articles on Clark Ashton Smith, and edited *Strange Shadows*, *The Unexpurgated Smith* series, and Smith's *Letters to H. P. Lovecraft*. His other interests include the fiction of J. G. Ballard and the New Wave, Stapledon, M. John Harrison, Mark S. Geston, Donald Wandrei, and William Gibson, the artwork of science-fiction illustrator Paul Lehr, and minimalist music.

www.ingramcontent.com/pod-product-compliance
Lightning Source LLC
LaVergne TN
LVHW041615070426
835507LV00008B/262